D1007957

The
WORST-CASE SCENARIO
Survival Handbook:
PARENTING

The
WORST-CASE SCENARIO
Survival Handbook:
PARENTING

By Joshua Piven, David Borgenicht, and Sarah Jordan
Illustrations by Brenda Brown

CHRONICLE BOOKS

SAN FRANCISCO

Copyright © 2003 by Quirk Productions, Inc.

All rights reserved. No part of this book may be reproduced in any form without written permission from the publisher.

Worst-Case Scenario™ and The Worst-Case Scenario Survival Handbook™ are trademarks of Quirk Productions, Inc.

Library of Congress Cataloging-in-Publication Data available.

ISBN: 0-8118-4155-3

Manufactured in the United States of America

Typeset in Adobe Caslon, Bundesbahn Pi, and Zapf Dingbats

Designed by Frances J. Soo Ping Chow
Illustrations by Brenda Brown

A **QUIRK** Book
www.quirkpackagimg.com
Visit www.worstcasescenarios.com

Distributed in Canada by Raincoast Books
9050 Shaughnessy Street
Vancouver, British Columbia V6P 6E5

10 9 8 7 6 5 4 3 2

Chronicle Books LLC
85 Second Street
San Francisco, California 94105
www.chroniclebooks.com

WARNING

When a life is imperiled or a dire situation is at hand, safe alternatives may not exist. To deal with the parenting worst-case scenarios presented in this book, we highly recommend—insist, actually—that the best course of action is to consult a professionally trained expert. But because highly trained professionals may not always be available when the safety or sanity of individuals is at risk, we have asked experts on various subjects to describe the techniques they might employ in these emergency situations. THE PUBLISHER, AUTHORS, AND EXPERTS DISCLAIM ANY LIABILITY from any injury that may result from the use, proper or improper, of the information contained in this book. We do not guarantee that the information contained herein is complete, safe, or accurate, nor should it be considered a substitute for your good judgment, your common sense, or your mother's advice. And finally, nothing in this book should be construed or interpreted to infringe on the rights of other persons or to violate criminal statutes; we urge you to obey all laws and respect all rights, including property rights, of others, even children.

—The Authors

CONTENTS

I was a much better parent
before I had children.

—Anonymous

INTRODUCTION

Four out of five survival experts agree that the most perilous worst-case scenarios are not the ones that involve wild animals attacking, large machines malfunctioning, or Mother Nature getting angry. Sharks, runaway trains, and avalanches are not the real dangers—humans are.

And of all human beings, those posing the greatest risk are *children*.

This means that *parents* face the greatest dangers on earth. They face them not for the short duration it takes to escape from a car sinking in a river or to leap from building to building, but for years and years, sometimes as long as two decades. Just when parents think they might be getting a grip on dealing with the worst-case situations presented by an infant, the kid is a toddler, and then ten, and then a teen, each age requiring a whole new set of survival skills. This endurance contest; this emotional, physical, and financial marathon; this epic of survival, is parenthood.

For as long as there have been people on Earth, there have been parents and children, and still parenting hasn't really become any easier or less dangerous. Sure, some problems went away when families moved out of caves, but new problems arose when the teenager borrowed the car. As a result, classic child-rearing advice has been outstripped by developments in culture and technology, and also by the evolution of parent-resistant strains of children.

Hence the indisputable need for this survival handbook for you, the parent.

We have approached the subject of parenthood chronologically, beginning with the time your child is born and stopping with the time he or she leaves home (and providing you with ways to ensure your child doesn't move back in). The first section covers ages zero to three, with advice on how to deal with a screaming baby on an airplane, how to babyproof the house, and how to control a stroller in extreme conditions. The next section will help you navigate the years from three to twelve, with step-by-step instructions for removing a wad of paper from your child's nose, retrieving a child stuck in a tree, recapitating a doll, and surviving a soccer Saturday. The final section addresses the teenage years, including how to survive your child's first date, first driving lesson, musical preferences, and provocative clothing.

The appendix is essential to understanding teenage slang and instant-messaging codes, and also offers a comprehensive list of parental clichés and a concise "the birds and the bees" speech.

As in our previous *Worst-Case Scenario Survival Handbooks*, we've assembled a team of experts to offer guidance. Attorneys, circus clowns, family therapists, chewing gum manufacturers, emergency room physicians, flight attendants, security consultants, and bike racers help us help you determine the course of action, no matter how dangerous or perplexing the situation.

To be sure, there's nothing more rewarding than parenting: To give your child love, to watch your child develop, to teach skills that will help him or her have a healthy and happy childhood is amazingly fulfilling. To sneak into your child's room after your child has blissfully dropped off to sleep, to listen to the gentle breathing, to watch your child peacefully rest, is truly a joyous moment of parenthood.

This book is for all those other moments, when your child is not asleep.

—The Authors

CHAPTER 1

ZERO TO THREE

HOW TO DEAL WITH A SCREAMING BABY ON AN AIRPLANE

1 Make highly visible efforts to quiet your child.
Passengers and flight attendants will not be as upset with you if they think that you are doing everything you can. Talk to your child, sing to him, and bounce him; offer him a bottle, pacifier, or food; rock him; walk him up and down the aisles; distract him with the air safety card, airsickness bags, or in-flight phone. Do everything you can think of to calm your baby, and do it loudly and noticeably.

2 Create confusion and distraction.
If your child has not quieted down, act crazy. Cross your eyes; make the "beebeebeebeebeebeebeebee" sound by moving your finger up and down between your lips; sing, preferably an aria, at full volume—do anything you can to distract your child from his tantrum. Then soothe him using more traditional methods.

3 Do not panic if your child will still not calm down.
Remember that this is only a moment in time, and that no matter how many nasty looks you are getting from fellow passengers, you are doing the best you can.

Tell yourself you will never see these people again.

4 Use drugs and alcohol.

Certain over-the-counter drugs can be administered in an emergency situation. Cold or allergy medicine for children, in particular, works well and usually causes drowsiness and a calming feeling. However, the medication may take half an hour or longer to take effect, and it frequently produces the opposite effect on children, speeding them up. The alcohol is for your consumption, in appropriate doses.

5 Use the lavatory.

If your child still will not calm down, retreat to the lavatory with him until he exhausts himself. Hold the baby in front of the mirror and say, "There's another baby in the room!" or pretend that you are "walking downstairs" by moving back and forth in the lavatory, stooping lower with each step.

6 Bribe fellow passengers for forgiveness.
Offer free drinks, extra bags of snacks, earplugs, and reimbursement for dry-cleaning expenses.

7 Remind yourself that you will never see these people again.
Repeat.

Be Aware
- First-class and business-class passengers usually have less tolerance for screaming babies.
- Do not pretend you do not know the child. Laws regarding child abandonment and neglect are more troublesome than annoyed passengers.

IF YOU ARE OUT OF DIAPERS

1 Ask the flight attendant for several cloth napkins.
Cloth napkins make an excellent temporary diaper.

2 Fold two cloth napkins into rectangles.

3 Place the two folded napkins (the liner) in the center of a third cloth napkin (the diaper).

4 Secure as you would a normal cloth diaper.
Effective fasteners include safety pins, bobby pins, hair clips, or butterfly-style binder clips. Use for short periods only, since the starch in the napkins may irritate the baby's skin.

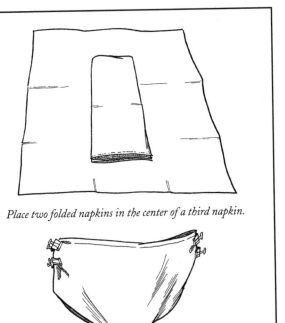

Place two folded napkins in the center of a third napkin.

Butterfly-style binder clips are effective fasteners.

Be Aware

The following items should not be used in place of a diaper:

- Silk scarf
- Wool blanket
- Suede jacket
- Baseball cap
- Straw hat
- Flotation device

HOW TO MAKE
AN EMERGENCY
BOTTLE

⭐ Use a medicine dropper or turkey baster.
Dribble milk (or formula or other liquid) into the side of the baby's mouth. Allow time for swallowing before inserting the next dropperful.

⭐ Use a straw.
Suck fluid into a straw and sustain tension by placing your thumb on the top of the straw. Put the straw into the side of the baby's mouth and remove your thumb periodically from the straw, releasing the tension and allowing the liquid to dribble out at intervals.

⭐ Use a gravy boat.
Slowly pour small amounts of liquid into the baby's mouth with the spout directing intake. Small creamers from tea sets can also be used. Even better are creamers from children's tea sets.

⭐ Use a water gun.
Fill the barrel with milk. Gently pull the trigger and squirt milk into the side of the baby's mouth.

⭐ Use a sports water bottle.
Squeeze milk into the baby's mouth.

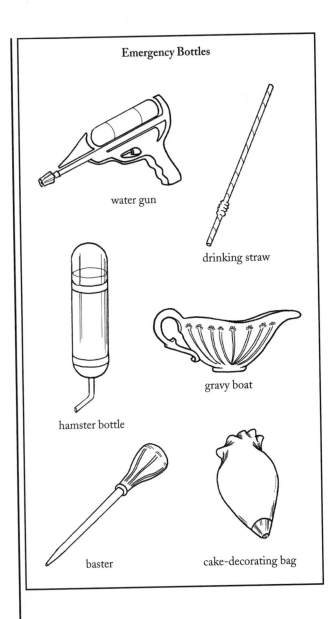

Emergency Bottles

water gun

drinking straw

hamster bottle

gravy boat

baster

cake-decorating bag

how to make an emergency bottle

Use a cake-decorating bag.

Fill the bag three-quarters full with milk, keeping your finger over the hole of the decorating tip. Twist the end of the bag and hold it closed to contain the milk. Gingerly insert the tip into the baby's mouth at regular intervals and control the flow of the milk with your fingertip. Round, oval, and leaf decorating tips are preferred.

Use a hamster bottle.

Sterilize the bottle and tube. Fill the bottle with milk. The leakproof vacuum will prevent the milk from spilling. Do not secure the bottle onto a car seat or bassinet for self-feeding.

Be Aware

Do not use airplane mini-bottles or rubber gloves or balloons with a hole poked in the end as substitute bottles.

HOW TO GIVE YOUR BABY A BATH WITHOUT A BATHTUB

You will need: soap, shampoo, bath toys, washcloth, cotton balls, hooded towel, and a post-bath diaper.

1 Select a location/container.
Acceptable locations include:
- Sink
- Roasting pan
- Large plastic container or bowl
- Litter box (empty and clean)
- Fish tank
- Ocean
- City fountain
- Koi pond

DO NOT USE:
- Drive-through car wash (with open car windows)
- Toilet bowl
- Front-loading washing machines
- Outdoor power sprayer
- Dishwasher
- Hot tub

2 Line the bottom of the container with a towel.
Use towels to prevent the baby from slipping and to add cushioning for comfort.

Brace the baby with your non-washing hand.

3 Fill the receptacle with warm water.
Check the temperature with your wrist or elbow before placing the baby in the water. Keep the room where the baby is bathing warm.

4 Undress the baby.

5 Place the baby in the bathing receptacle.

6 Support the child while washing.
Brace younger children with your non-washing hand. Introduce a makeshift bath toy such as plastic measuring spoons or a small ball. Do not offer the child measuring cups or other objects that can be used to bail out the tub.

7 Rinse.
Rinse the baby with a wet washcloth frequently dipped in clean water and squeezed over the baby. Alternatively, you can use water from a pitcher, but make sure it has not cooled past comfort levels. Do not attempt to rinse the baby by pouring water if the basin is full.

8 Remove the baby and dry.
Wrap the baby in a soft towel and pat dry immediately to keep her warm.

Be Aware
- Keep soap out of an infant's eyes while washing her hair by tilting her head back and placing a small washcloth on her forehead. Do not hold the washcloth in place or shield her eyes with your hand since you will need that hand to support the baby while the other hand washes and rinses. When the child is a little older, you can use a terry-cloth headband, bandanna, or tiny golf visor to shield the eyes from soap or shampoo.
- For spot cleaning, use a water gun, saline solution squirted from a bottle, or a spray bottle. A drinking fountain can also be used to rinse a slightly dirty baby when the target area can be positioned under the arc of water and when the water is not too cold.
- Do not wash the baby with wipes. What's good for the bottom can be too harsh for the rest of the body.

HOW TO GET YOUR BABY TO SLEEP

⭐ Swaddle the baby.

Fold down one corner of a receiving blanket and place the baby on top of the blanket with his head above the fold. Pull one side of the blanket securely across the baby's chest and tuck it underneath his body. Then pull up the bottom, folding the edge back, and finish by pulling the remaining side of the blanket across the baby's chest and underneath the body. The baby should fit snugly inside the blanket.

⭐ Sway.

Hold the swaddled baby close to your chest. Shift your weight from one foot to the other. This rhythmic stimulation will induce a sleepy state in the baby. Position the child so that his ear is over your heart. The beating will soothe him.

⭐ Generate soothing white noise near the baby.

Sound produced by a clothes dryer, dishwasher, blender, coffee grinder, hair dryer, vacuum cleaner, lawn mower, leaf blower, or air conditioner has a lulling potency that many babies cannot resist. Metronomes and ticking clocks can also soothe a baby to sleep by reminding a child of his mother's heart beat.

⭐ **Put the baby on a washing machine or dryer.**
Turn on the machine and set to normal cycle. The vibrations and noise are sleep-inducing. Do not leave the baby unattended.

⭐ **Go for a drive.**
The steady vibration of the car will have most infants asleep quickly. Open the window a crack and the air will keep you awake while the sound of the wind functions as soothing white noise for the baby. Do not get behind the wheel if you are exhausted and cannot operate heavy machinery.

Vibrations from a washer or dryer are sleep-inducing.

✪ Dance to music with a strong beat.
Hold the child securely in your arms and bounce, twirl, and dip in a rhythmic fashion. Concentrate on moving the baby to the beat. The nonstop, steady jiggling will overload the brain's processing center. Avoid atonal, early-twentieth-century classical music, bebop, or any other music that could be jarring. Better choices include reggae, house, dance/trance, disco, minimalist, and pop.

✪ Climb up and down a staircase.
Make sure your grip is tight around the baby. Go up and down at a rapid, steady pace.

✪ Use a pacifier.
A pacifier (also known as a binky, paci, dummy, comforter, fooler, ninny, soother, soothie, or yum yum) can be an extraordinarily potent sleep inducer for some babies, but it can be habit-forming, and may cause problems if lost or stolen.

DO NOT USE AS A PACIFIER

bottle

cell phone

screwdriver

toilet plunger handle

high-heel shoe

salt or pepper shaker

lightbulb

Ping-Pong paddle

how to get your baby to sleep

HOW TO PROTECT YOURSELF FROM UNWANTED WETNESS

⭐ Drape a burp cloth on each shoulder.
Shoulders are the primary repository for baby's wetness. Cover each shoulder with a diaper or burping cloth (if unavailable, remove shoulder pads from your clothes, if you have them, and wear them on the outside). Do not pin the protective cloth to your shoulder, since the pin could scratch the baby.

⭐ Secure your hair.
Pull long hair back and away from the baby's grasping, food-smeared fingers. Wrap a ponytail into a bun on top of your head. Do not use pins, clips, or bands, which the baby can remove, to secure hair. Try a hairnet, bell cap, or ski mask for complete protection.

⭐ Wear recreational spectacles.
Use swimming goggles, laboratory goggles, or other protective eye gear to keep baby food, fluids, and fingers out of your eyes. Use strap-on eyewear, which is more difficult for the baby to remove than regular rest-on-ear glasses.

⭐ Wear a smock.
Use a large, old shirt, worn backwards.

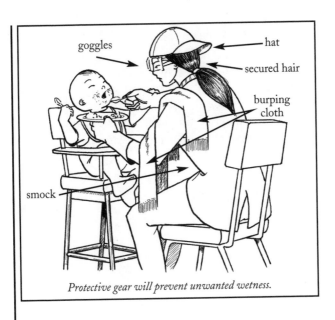

Protective gear will prevent unwanted wetness.

⭐ Wear a bath towel.
Cut a hole in the middle of the towel for your head.
Roll back the edges of the incision and finish the
edges to prevent unraveling.

⭐ Wear an additional layer of clothing.
Surgical scrubs or oversized pajamas provide comprehensive protection, are easy to put on and remove, and
are easily washable.

⭐ Wear nothing.
Particularly when feeding a messy eater, wear as little
clothing as possible. Take a quick communal bath
afterwards.

★ Keep a firm grip on your baby's ankles when changing a diaper.

Maintain a tight but gentle clasp of both ankles. Allowing even one ankle to go free in mid–diaper change will provide the baby with the opportunity to slam his heel down to the surface of the changing area and into the contents of his soiled diaper.

★ Make a barrier when changing your son's diaper.

Place a diaper or burp cloth on his lower abdomen after you remove the old diaper. The protective cloth will guard against a potential fountain.

HOW TO BABYPROOF THE HOUSE

1 Crawl around on your hands and knees to see the house from your child's point of view.
Anticipate the things that will interest him.

2 Remove all sharp edges.
Create corner bumpers out of foam or bubble wrap. Protect all hard edges within the child's reach, including coffee tables, end tables, bookcases, televisions, entertainment centers, hard chairs, dressers, bed stands, and desks.

3 Protect electrical outlets.
Use spring-loaded release covers in electrical outlets; plastic slip-in outlet guards can be too easily removed. Alternatively, move electrical outlets higher on the wall, to just below the ceiling, or replace all electrical appliances with battery-operated appliances. Batteries are toxic, however.

4 Install window guards.
Use window guards that prevent windows from opening more than 4 inches. Use the sliding button guard or the lock-and-key guard (which also keeps burglars out, but might prohibit a fast exit in an emergency). Protect low-to-the-ground windows with a hard plastic sheet or soft Mylar coating that prevents a child from shattering the glass. Do not use tilt-out windows

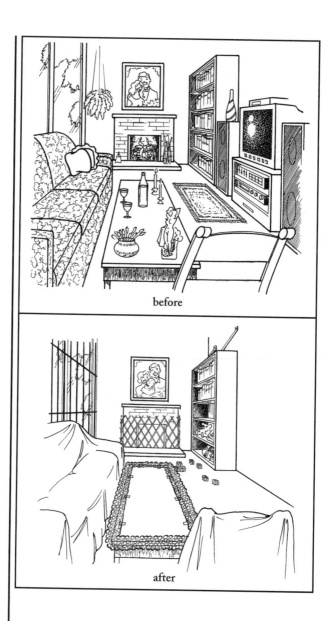

before

after

unless windows are kept closed and locked at all times. Alternatively, install bars not more than 2⅜ inches apart on the outside of windows.

5 Install childproof doorknob spinners.
Deter your child from entering unsafe rooms or closets by covering all doorknobs with childproof covers that will spin loosely when a child attempts to turn the knob.

6 Install drawer and cabinet guards.
To prevent your child from reaching knives in a drawer or cleaning agents under the sink, secure drawers and cabinets with childproof latches.

7 Hang towels over the top of doors to prevent the child from slamming the door on his fingers.
Alternatively, remove all doors.

8 Bolt heavy furniture to walls.
Tall, heavy furniture can be tipped and pulled down by children, especially if they are climbing. Strap or secure bookcases, dressers, cabinets, and televisions. Tape lamps to tables or floors.

9 Avoid entanglements.
Tie up (or down) or remove all curtains, blinds, and cords, especially electrical cords.

10 Remove poisonous plants.
If you are not sure which plants are poisonous, throw them all away. Eliminate hazardous outdoor plants as well as houseplants.

11 Install baby gates.

Use gates that are 30 inches tall and have only vertical posts, with a bar top and bottom: Do not use diamond-shaped accordion gates that a child can climb. Place a gate at the top and bottom of a staircase. Keep gates closed at all times, even when the baby is asleep or not home.

12 Block the fireplace.

Put a nontoxic plant or fake logs in the grate. Install a gate around the outside of the hearth to prevent the child from approaching the fireplace or from sustaining an injury after hitting the edge of the fireplace. Put away all fireplace tools. Do not use the fireplace for actual fires until the child is older.

13 Reduce the temperature of the hot water heater.

Turn the water heater to 120°F or below to prevent scalding.

14 Install a spout guard over the bathtub spigot.

Mount foam on the metal faucet to prevent inadvertent head gouging or bumping while bathing.

15 Install a stove guard.

Attach a plastic shield in front of your stove's burners to prevent your child from reaching up and overturning pots and pans or burning fingers on hot or flaming surfaces. Affix knob protectors so your child cannot accidentally turn on the range.

Do not allow the baby to watch a dog drinking from the toilet.

16 Put lid guards on all toilets.

Do not let the baby watch a dog drink from the toilet bowl.

17 Line floors with gym mats.

Cover all flat surfaces with gym mats several inches thick to provide extra padding in case of a fall.

Be Aware

Keep purses and diaper bags, which are repositories for dangerous items and choking hazards, out of the reach of children. Put away guests' bags as well.

HOW TO MAKE EMERGENCY TOYS

⭐ Turn objects into faces.
Socks, spoons, pillows, plates—any object can become a fascinating toy when you give it eyes, a nose, and a mouth. Funny voices that appear to come from the object also add appeal.

⭐ Add sound.
Place coins, beans, rocks, keys, or other small objects inside a sippy cup or plastic storage container to create an instant rattle or musical instrument. Make certain the lid is tightly fastened to avoid potential choking hazards.

⭐ Create pairs.
Tie together two objects, like wooden spoons or shoes, with a short string. When the baby pulls one, the other follows, or when she knocks one off a table, the other falls, too. This cause-and-effect game sharpens a baby's motor skills and provides hours of fun.

AIRPLANE TELEPHONE

1 Remove the phone from the seat back in front of you.

2 Hand your child the phone.

3 Say, "See if you can call someone."

4 Watch the button pushing and conversation.
As long as you don't have a credit card in the phone, there's no activation and no charge.

5 Discontinue the game if she becomes frustrated.
Also discontinue if your neighbors become annoyed.

AIRPLANE AIRSICKNESS BAG PUPPET

1 Remove the airsickness bag from the seat pocket in front of you.
Verify that the bag is empty.

2 Draw eyes on the bottom of the bag.

3 Lift the edge of the bottom slightly and add a tongue.
This will be the mouth.

4 Place your hand inside the bag.

5 Animate.

RESTAURANT NAPKIN

1 Obtain a paper napkin.
Ask your server for an extra napkin, or borrow one from a nearby table.

2 Open the napkin fully.

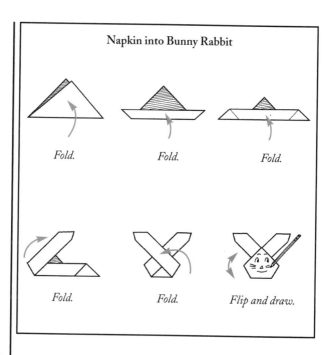

Napkin into Bunny Rabbit

Fold. *Fold.* *Fold.*

Fold. *Fold.* *Flip and draw.*

3 Fold it into a triangle.

4 Fold the longest side up approximately 1.5 inches.

5 Fold the same side the same amount again.

6 Fold one end of the bottom edge toward the center, on a diagonal, to form one of the ears.

7 Repeat with the other bottom edge.

8 Hold the napkin in place, and flip it over.

9 Draw a bunny rabbit face.

10 Play.
Tape the bunny's head to a spoon to make it into a stick puppet.

EVERYDAY ITEMS

Readily available items can be repurposed to entertain small children in an emergency.

- Tongue depressors—pickup sticks, dancing puppets.
- Rubber gloves—inflatable turkeys.
- Phonograph—merry-go-round for small dolls or animals.
- Funnel—megaphone, trumpet.
- Banana—telephone.
- Orange—soccer ball.
- Spice bottle—rattle.
- Tissue box—box of birds.
- CDs—ring toss.
- Wooden spoons and plastic containers—drums, twirling circus.

Be Aware
- Keep a toy everywhere—in the car, in the stroller (or tied to it), in the diaper bag, in the backpack—to avoid being caught without one.
- Purchase a backup of your child's favorite toy. The treasured toy will eventually get lost or broken.

HOW TO CONTROL A STROLLER IN EXTREME CONDITIONS

SNOW AND ICE

1 Wear hiking boots.
Put on boots or shoes with rubber soles and thick treads for good traction. Avoid high heels and shoes with smooth leather soles.

2 Add ballast.
Place full formula bottles, bricks, or books over the stroller's wheels to provide added stability and traction.

3 Keep one foot firmly planted.
Walk so that at least one foot has good traction continuously. If you begin to slide, slow down.

4 Hold the handles firmly.

5 Avoid sharp turns and sudden movements.

6 Steer into the slide.
If the stroller begins to slide, bend your knees and steer into the slide. Avoid sudden corrective measures that may make the stroller harder to control or cause a spin-out.

7 Do not lean on the stroller.
A stroller will not support the weight of an adult. Leaning on the stroller for balance may propel the wheels across the ice and cause you to lose your balance and control.

8 Abandon the stroller only in case of severe emergency.
If you must abandon the stroller, use downed tree branches to mark the spot for recovery later. Remove the baby and other necessary items.

Down a Steep Hill

1 Assess the slope.
Do not roll children in strollers down a hill steeper than 30 degrees. If the hill looks very steep, or if you have trouble maintaining your footing, choose another path.

2 Check the safety belt.
Buckle the stroller's safety belt snugly against the child, but not so tight that it causes pain.

3 Secure any loose items.
Bottles, books, and toys stored in stroller pockets or in the basket underneath may come loose during the descent. Use spare diapers to wedge these items in place, or leave them behind.

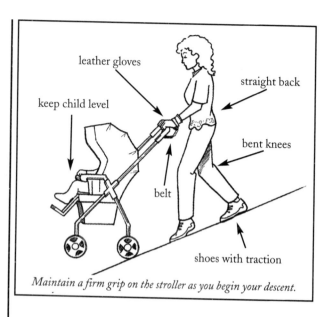

Maintain a firm grip on the stroller as you begin your descent.

4 Maintain your grip.
Firmly hold both handles of the stroller at all times. If your hands are sweaty, dry them with a burping cloth before descent. Wear leather driving gloves to increase grip: Do not wear ski mittens, which are slippery.

5 Lift up the front wheels.
Angle the stroller so that the child stays level and does not pitch forward.

6 Begin the descent.
Move slowly, keeping your knees bent and your back straight. Avoid leaning forward or you risk toppling onto the stroller.

7   Adjust the angle of the child and stroller.
If the child is pitching forward, put additional downward pressure on the handles and angle the front wheels further toward the sky.

8   Rest periodically.
If you become tired, turn the stroller uphill so that the child faces toward the crest of the hill, and stand below it, facing the same direction. Apply the parking brake. Keep your legs straight while in this resting position.

Be Aware
For added safety, remove your belt and lash your wrist to one of the handles of the stroller or to the handle bar. Wrap the belt several times around your wrist and then around the handle, then fasten the buckle.

DO NOT USE A STROLLER . . .

as a shopping cart

as a sidecar

as a scooter/skateboard

when running with the bulls in Pamplona

how to control a stroller in extreme conditions

HOW TO REPAIR A BROKEN STROLLER

DAMAGED CANOPY

 Patch.

- UMBRELLA STROLLER—Pull the damaged section taut. Sew a ripped or torn cloth canopy with needle and thread. Use duct or electrical tape to repair a plastic or vinyl canopy.
- CARRIAGE STROLLER—Canopies on larger, carriage-type strollers are generally sturdier, with plastic frames that rotate on hinges to cover the baby in various positions. Check the hinges (there should be one on each side of the stroller) where the canopy attaches to the stroller frame. If the canopy has come off its hinge, try to snap it back in place. If the hinge is damaged, secure the canopy to the stroller frame using string, yarn, a belt, or a purse strap.

 Construct a makeshift canopy.
If the canopy cannot be repaired, place a shirt or other lightweight piece of material on the canopy frame and secure in place using string, tape, rubber bands, or hair clips. This will protect the baby from the elements temporarily.

Be Aware

In inclement weather, position an open umbrella in place of the canopy to keep the baby dry. Make sure the metal frame of the umbrella is far enough from the baby to be out of reach.

BROKEN STRAP

⭐  Pin the strap together.

A strap or safely belt that has torn in two can be reconnected using two small safety pins or one large diaper pin. Take the baby out of the stroller while you perform the repair.

⭐ Tie the ends with a square knot.

If there is enough slack, tie the two broken ends together with a square knot. Holding one end of the broken strap in each hand, pass the left over the right, and tuck under. Then pass the same end, now in the right hand, over the left, and tuck under. Pull the ends together tightly for added security.

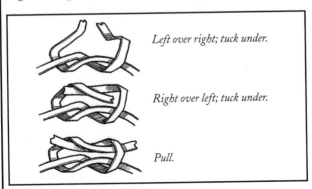

Left over right; tuck under.

Right over left; tuck under.

Pull.

☆ Substitute your own belt.

Use an adult's belt to hold the child in the stroller. Run the belt across the child's lap and around the back of the stroller. Buckle the belt behind the stroller.

FAULTY BRAKES

☆ Disengage the brake.

- **PEDAL OR BAR BRAKE**—On standard strollers, the brakes are activated by pressing down on a pedal or bar above the rear wheels. A faulty brake will not stay in the raised position and will continue engaging, thereby stopping the wheels from turning. Use rubber bands, string, or twist-ties to attach the pedal or bar to the legs of the stroller: This will prevent it from falling and engaging the wheels. Make sure the connection is tight and there is no slippage.
- **HAND BRAKE**—Three-wheeled jogging strollers may have a hand brake, operated by squeezing a handle that pulls a cable, as on a bike. If the brake cable is broken, the brake will clamp the wheels and prevent them from turning. Pull the two ends of the wire together until the wire is taut. Twist the ends together for a temporary fix.

HOW TO CONSTRUCT AN EMERGENCY CRIB

Parents' bed.

Remove pillows and other loose items and put them on the floor around the base of the bed. Add additional pillows, sofa cushions, comforters, and spare blankets until the height of the surrounding pile reaches to within six inches, at least, of the top of the bed. The pillows will create a soft landing area if the baby wanders.

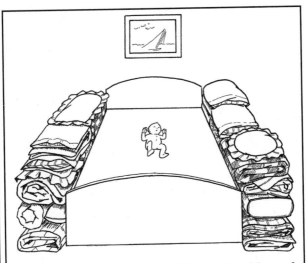

Pile extra blankets and cushions to within six inches of the top of your bed to create a soft landing area.

★ Storage bin.
Place an under-the-bed (half-height) plastic storage bin in the center of the room. Do not place under your own bed. Pad as necessary.

★ Dresser drawer.
Remove a drawer from a dresser and line with crib sheets and cotton blanket. Place on the floor.

★ Laundry basket.
Line a large basket with soft blankets or comforters.

★ Wagon.
Pad a child-sized wagon with blankets. Lock the wheels or wedge them with books to prevent rolling.

Be Aware

- In a regular or an improvised crib, pillows and other loose items may present a suffocation danger. Do not place small, sharp, heavy, electrical, or sporting objects in a crib. Also keep food, beverages, and pets out of the crib.
- Makeshift cribs must be monitored at all times.

DO NOT PUT IN A CRIB

how to construct an emergency crib

HOW TO SURVIVE BABY-GEAR OVERLOAD

1 Wear cargo pants.
Fill the pockets with soft items:
- Burp cloth
- Bibs
- Change of clothes (for you and for baby)

2 Dress the baby in cargo pants.
Fill the pockets with small necessities:
- Baby's cap
- Small board book for entertainment
- Teething ring

3 Wear a photographer's or fisherman's vest.
Fill the pockets with necessities:
- Small camera and film
- Baby blanket
- Crib toy
- Baby manual
- Hand sanitizer
- Bowl and spoon
- Changing pad
- Shampoo
- Nail clippers
- Bath soap
- Fever-reducing medicine

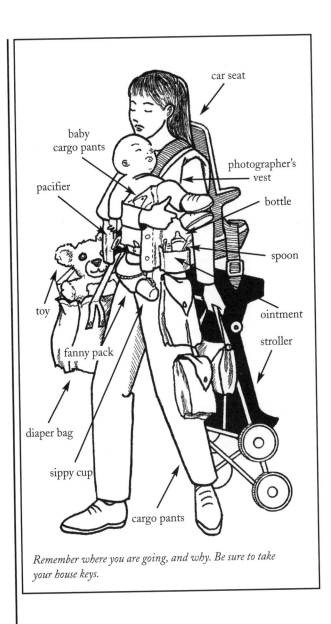

car seat

baby
cargo pants

photographer's
vest

pacifier

bottle

spoon

toy

ointment

fanny pack

stroller

diaper bag

sippy cup

cargo pants

*Remember where you are going, and why. Be sure to take
your house keys.*

- Teething gel
- Anti-itch cream
- Saline drops
- Nasal bulb syringe
- Thermometer
- Tissues
- Meat tenderizer for bee stings
- Adhesive bandages
- Antibiotic ointment
- Toothbrush and paste
- Plastic bag for soiled diapers
- Plastic bag for wet/dirty clothes

4 Wear a fanny pack.
Fill with adult necessities:
- Keys
- Wallet
- Headache medicine
- Sunglasses
- Makeup
- Cell phone
- Shopping list
- Pen

5 Circle your waist with a web belt.
Attach a canteen (for you) and a bottle or sippy cup (for baby).

6 Clip a pacifier to the baby.

7 | Sling a messenger bag across your back.
Fill with remaining necessities:
- Umbrella
- Toys
- Diapers
- Diaper wipes
- Cotton balls
- Sunscreen
- Diaper cream
- Juice
- Crackers
- Video camera

8 | Wear a baby carrier or sling.
Place the baby in the carrier and go. Remember where you are going, and why, and be sure to take your house keys with you.

HOW TO BREAK INTO YOUR CAR IF YOUR BABY IS LOCKED INSIDE

1 Maintain visual contact with your baby.
Observe her medical condition. Trick your baby into thinking that you meant to create this situation. See "How to Keep Your Baby Calm" on the following page.

2 Try a key from a similar model of car.
Ask passersby if they drive the same type of car. Ask if they will try to open your door with their key.

3 Use a coat hanger to break in.
Bend a wire hanger into a long J. Square off the bottom of the J so that the square is about two inches wide. Slide the hanger into the door, between the window and the weather stripping. Feel for the end of the button rod and, when you have it, pull it up to open the lock.

4 Break the window.
Don a pair of gloves, mittens, or socks to protect your hands from abrasion and injury. Select the window farthest from your child—a front window is ideal. Use a sharp object to punch through the middle of the window—try a rock, hammer, crowbar, piece of concrete from a broken curb, or even a low concrete parking-

spot marker. Hit the window with enough force to break the surface tension on the glass. Do not use your fist or a blunt object, neither of which will break the glass.

5 Call for help.
Police officers and firefighters sometimes carry keys or lock-pick tools, or call a locksmith. A professional can often spring the lock in as little as three seconds with no damage to your car.

Be Aware
- In cold weather, do not warm up the car with the child inside. Many new cars automatically lock the doors once the ignition is turned on.
- Larger glass panels are less expensive to replace than fixed panels, such as small quarter panels.

HOW TO KEEP YOUR BABY CALM

⭐ Pretend to be calm yourself.
The baby will feed off of your fear if you reveal it.

⭐ Play peek-a-boo.
Begin with the standard hands-in-front-of-face style, then try hiding your face with a scarf or hat, and finally pop up from below various windows.

⭐ Enlist the help of passersby.
Select friendly-looking people and people with babies who can coo at your baby through the window. Keep your child entertained and happy.

⭐ Hoist a small dog in front of a window.
Turn the dog around to show its funny wagging tail.

⭐ Hold up a magazine.
Turn the pages in front of the window so baby can see bright images.

⭐ Use makeup to color yourself like a clown.
Smear lipstick on lips (go beyond true lip outline), cheeks, and tip of nose. Use eyeliner and eyeshadow to accentuate happy eyes and eyebrows.

⭐ Do vigorous calisthenics.
Babies think it's funny to see big people jump around.

Enlist the help of passersby to keep your child entertained.

HOW TO SAVE FOR COLLEGE

A four-year public college education (including room and board, excluding taxes and activity expenses) in the United States will cost approximately $155,000 in 2020. A four-year private college education (including room and board) will cost approximately $335,000. Here are some ways to pay for your newborn's education:

⭐ Save money.
Squirrel away $23.60 a day for public school or $51 a day for private school.

⭐ Recycle.
At 5 cents a can you will need to recycle 3,100,000 cans to pay for public school and 6,700,000 cans for private school.

⭐ Sell lemonade.
At 20 cents a cup your lemonade stand will need to sell 775,000 cups to pay for public school and 1,675,000 cups for private school.

⭐ Hold a bake sale.
At $1.75 for a (cranberry-walnut) muffin, you will need to bake and sell 88,571 muffins to pay for public school and 191,429 muffins for private school. (Cost of ingredients not included.)

Sell lemonade.

Pose as a model.

⭐ Pose as a model.
At $8 an hour to pose nude for art students, you will need to sit for 19,375 hours (about two and a half years) to pay for public school and 41,875 hours (about four and a half years) for private school.

⭐ Babysit.
At $10 an hour you will need to sit for 15,500 hours (about a year and a half) to pay for public school or 33,500 hours (nearly four years) to pay for private school.

⭐ Walk dogs.
At $15 a walk (30 minutes) for one dog, you will need to walk 10,333 dogs to pay for public school and 22,333 dogs for private school.

⭐ Fish sit.
At $9 a visit to maintain an aquarium you will need to see 17,222 tanks to pay for public school or 37,222 tanks to pay for private school.

⭐ Clean rain gutters.
If you are paid $20 each time you clean a home's rain gutters, you will have to clean 7,750 homes to pay for public school and 16,750 homes for private school.

⭐ Mow lawns.
If the rate is approximately $40 a lawn, you will have to mow 3,875 lawns to pay for public school and 8,375 lawns to pay for private school.

★ Rake leaves.

If you receive $50 an acre, you will need to rake 3,100 acres for public school and 6,700 acres for private school.

★ Groom pets.

If you receive $65 for an extra-large, long-hair dog (flea dip, clip, ears and teeth cleaned, nails clipped, anal glands checked), you will need to groom 2,385 dogs to pay for public school and 5,154 dogs for private school.

★ Bartend.

If you are working at a bar that generates $200 per night in tips, you will have to work 775 nights to pay for public school and 1,675 nights to pay for private school.

★ Sell hair.

At $5 an ounce for your hair, you will need to sell 1,938 pounds of hair to pay for public school and 4,188 pounds for private school.

★ Sell your egg or sperm.

At approximately $20,000 an egg, you will need to harvest and sell eight eggs to pay for public school and 17 eggs to pay for private school. At $50 a sperm sample, you will need 3,100 samples to pay for public school and 6,700 to pay for private school.

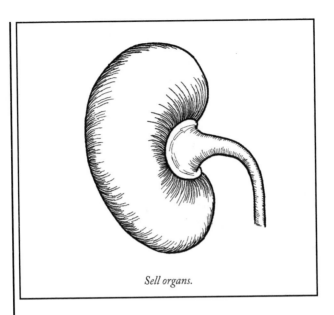

Sell organs.

 Sell organs.

At $30,000 a kidney on the black market, you will need five members of your immediate family to donate one kidney to pay for public school and eleven members of your immediate family to donate a kidney for private school.

Be Aware

- All savings plans, above, assume that earnings are not taxed. Additional amounts will need to be earned to cover taxes.
- All savings plans assume that earnings are not invested; interest, dividends, or appreciation on investments will contribute to earnings.

CHAPTER 2

THREE TO TWELVE

HOW TO REMOVE CHEWING GUM FROM HAIR

Using Ice

1 Prepare an ice sack.

Place several cubes of ice in a plastic bag or thin cloth. Seal or hold it closed.

2 Apply ice pack to hair.

Move the affected hair away from the scalp and press the ice against the gum for 15 to 30 minutes or until the gum freezes solid. Use a rubber glove or a dry washcloth to hold the ice compress if your hand becomes chilled.

3 Crack the frozen gum into pieces.

With one hand, hold the stuck section of the hair between the gum clot and the scalp, and break the frozen gum into small pieces.

4 Remove the gum.

Gently pull the frozen gum pieces from the hair using your other hand. If the warmth of your hand begins to melt the gum, refreeze and repeat until all the gum has been removed from the hair.

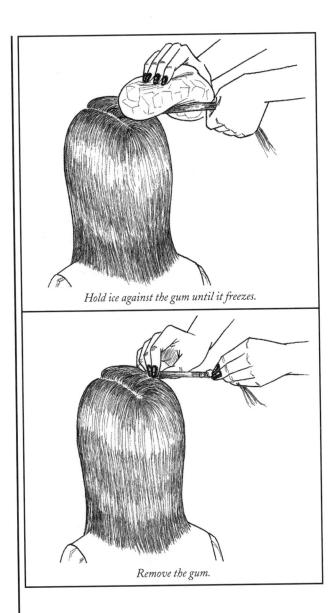

Hold ice against the gum until it freezes.

Remove the gum.

Using Oils

1 Rub a citrus-based solvent into the gum.
Cleaning products with oils from citrus fruit peels will reduce the stickiness of chewing gum and allow the hair to be pulled free. Apply a small amount of the solvent directly to the gum wad and rub until the hair can be separated without pain. Follow the solvent manufacturer's instructions and wear rubber gloves.

2 Loosen the gum with peanut butter.
If no solvent is available, the natural oils in peanut butter may loosen the gum. Work a teaspoon of peanut butter into the gum until the hair can be pulled free of the gum.

3 Apply mineral or cooking oil.
If the peanut butter is ineffective, work a very small amount of mineral or cooking oil into the gum to loosen it from the hair.

4 Wash and rinse.
Wash hair and hands with shampoo and soap to remove any lingering solvents, foods, or oils.

HOW TO REMOVE A WAD OF PAPER FROM YOUR CHILD'S NOSE

1 Pull gently on any protruding paper.
Pinch the paper firmly between your index finger and thumb. Pull with a steady downward motion until the wad comes free, taking care not to rip it. If the wad does not budge, or if no paper protrudes, continue to the next step.

2 Sterilize a pair of tweezers.
Rub them with hydrogen peroxide or isopropyl alcohol.

3 Tilt the child's head back to give you a clear view of the nostril and tissue wad.
Use a flashlight or desk lamp for better visibility. Hold the child's head steady.

4 Insert the tweezers into the nose.
Place the tip of the tweezers around as much of the paper wad as possible. Make certain the tweezers have a firm grasp on the paper wad or you risk tearing off small pieces and prolonging the job. Do not push the wad deeper into the nostril.

5 Pull steadily.
Do not yank the wad. Have a clean tissue or handkerchief ready to absorb any leakage.

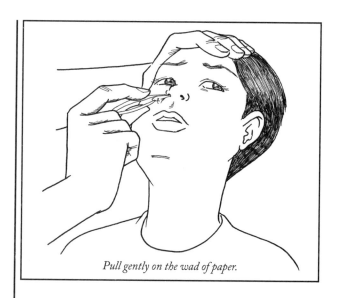

Pull gently on the wad of paper.

6 Discard the wad.
Wash hands thoroughly.

How to Remove a Pea, Marble, or Other Solid Object

1 Place your mouth over the child's mouth.
The position is the same as for mouth-to-mouth resuscitation.

2 Press the unclogged nostril closed with your finger.

3 Blow.
Blow a short but forceful puff into the child's mouth.
The stuck object should pop free.

HOW TO UNTIE A SEVERELY KNOTTED SHOELACE

1 Gently pull one end of the lace.
Tangles that appear to be knots may actually be a series of intertwined loops and bows, which are held in place by friction rather than by a knot. Pull a free end of the lace using minimal force. If the tangle is not truly knotted, it will come apart immediately.

2 Loosen from the center.
If the lace is knotted, begin by loosening from the center of the tangle.

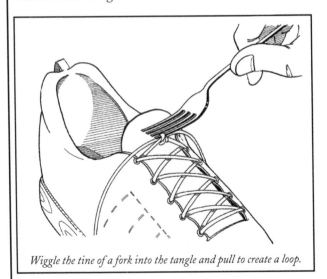

Wiggle the tine of a fork into the tangle and pull to create a loop.

3 Work slowly and patiently.

4 Do not yank.
Yanking on a loose end will not free the knot. It will make it worse. Be patient.

5 Insert a fork tine into the center of the knot.
Stubborn knots may be too tight for an adult's finger to manipulate. If the knot won't budge, wiggle the tine of a fork into the tangle and pull until a loop is created. Loosen one section, then repeat on the remaining sections of the knot.

HOW TO FIX A BROKEN SHOELACE

⭐ Connect broken strands.
Most laces have several inches of extra length. Tie the broken ends together using a square knot (see the diagram on page 49).

⭐ Use the longer strand.
If the lace broke near one end, discard the shorter section and relace using the longer strand. Wet and twist the ragged end to fit through eyelets.

⭐ Make a replacement lace.
Many children's jumpers or jackets have drawstrings. Pull the drawstring out—you may have to take out a knot at either end—and thread it through the shoe.

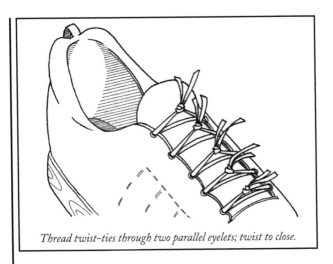

Thread twist-ties through two parallel eyelets; twist to close.

 Use twist-ties.

Twist-ties are relatively strong and will hold the sides of a shoe together temporarily. Thread the tie through two parallel eyelets on either side of the tongue and twist to close. Repeat until the shoe is secure.

Be Aware

- Nylon laces have less friction than string or cloth laces. Consider replacing string with nylon to ease knot removal.
- Step-in shoes without laces or untied shoes eliminate the knot problem.

HOW TO PREVENT BACKPACK OVERLOAD

1 Clean out the backpack.
Remove extra pairs of running shoes, soda bottles, CDs (if more than five), and all electronic games.

2 Pack only the necessary books.
All books do not need to go to and from school every day.

3 Buy a second set of books.
Keep a set of textbooks, usually the heaviest books, at home, so the books don't need to be transported. Alternatively, photocopy the entire book at the beginning of the year and instruct your child to take home only those pages necessary for each day's assignment.

4 Hire a neighborhood sherpa.
Pay a sibling, larger neighborhood child, or teamster to carry the load.

5 Affix saddlebags to your dog.
Bike stores usually sell a variety of different-sized bags that can be slung across a dog's back. Use only large dogs and watch for overload.

Pack only necessary books.

6 Ship the books overnight directly to school.

As long as your child completes his homework by 8 P.M., you should be able to ship the books for next-day delivery at a courier's local drop box. Specify that the books should arrive for "early delivery" to ensure that they make it to school before your child's first class of the day.

Be Aware

- A backpack should never rest 4 inches or more below the waistline or be wider than the shoulders.
- Symptoms of backpack overload include pain or numbness in the arms, shoulders, and mid- to lower back; jaw pain; neck pain; and headache. If the child reports any of these symptoms, consult a healthcare professional.

HOW TO DISCIPLINE AN IMAGINARY FRIEND

1 Outline responsibility.

Explain to your child and the imaginary friend that when they play together, they both need to be on good behavior and are both responsible for any broken vases, stolen cookies, or messes.

Explain to your child that both he and his imaginary friend are responsible for their bad behavior.

2 Assign consequences to the child and imaginary friend together.

Tell your child that he and his imaginary friend must wash dishes or take out the trash "together."

3 Ask your child to suggest ways to make his friend behave.

Explain that you need his help in making his friend understand and behave.

4 Create activities to keep the imaginary friend out of trouble.

If the imaginary friend is a continuing source of mischief, enroll him in (imaginary) music lessons, (imaginary) summer camp, or (imaginary) boarding school to keep him occupied.

Be Aware

- Do not make up an imaginary friend for your child as a way to encourage his imagination.
- Respond respectfully to your child's imagination and imaginary friend.
- If you are visiting someone, such as a boss, who may be uncomfortable with your child's notion, tell your child that his friend will have to wait in the car, or that you hired a "babysitter" for the child's friend to watch him at home.

HOW TO RECAPITATE A DOLL

Rag Doll

1 Restuff the head and torso.

If the neck area is mostly loose fabric and/or stuffing, use polyester fiberfill, available at craft stores, to replace lost stuffing. If fiberfill is unavailable, stuff nylon stockings into the head and neck areas.

2 Overlap the fabric of the head and neck slightly.

3 Sew the head to the neck.

Use standard-weight thread close to the color of the doll. Begin about $1/8$ inch from the initial stitch and sew three-quarters of the way around the doll's head.

Restuff the head and torso before reattaching the head.

4 Check the position of the head.
If the doll's head lolls to either side, use additional stuffing to stiffen its position.

5 Complete the sewing.
Stitching once around the neck should be sufficient to hold the head in place. Cut the thread and tie it off.

6 Hide the stitches with an accessory.
If the stitch work is unsightly, tie a colorful ribbon or bandanna around the doll's neck to conceal the surgery.

PLASTIC DOLL

1 Determine if the doll has a cuff joint at the nub.
Most plastic dolls have a cuff joint at the area where the head meets the neck. The nub is the part of the doll, either the neck or the top of the shoulders, that has separated from the head.

2 Heat the head.
Heating the plastic will make it pliable enough to re-insert into the cuff joint. Use a lighter or hair dryer on its highest setting to heat only the area of the head that fits over the nub. Heat for 2 minutes. Alternatively, boil a pot of water, remove from the heat, and let stand 1 minute, then submerge the affected part of the head for 2 minutes. Do not heat hair, eyebrows, or eyelashes.

Heat the head and then push it over the neck nub to snap it onto the body.

3 Push the head over the nub on the torso.

Work quickly, applying firm, steady pressure. Use a flathead screwdriver for added leverage, if necessary. The head should snap tightly onto the body.

4 Cool.

Allow the plastic to cool and reharden for several minutes before returning the doll to your child.

An 18-Inch Vinyl-headed Doll

1 Find the neck string.
The doll head is held in place by a string that runs through the neck casing at the top of the doll's body. The string will be visible where it comes out of the casing on the back of the body (where the back of the neck would be).

2 Untie the neck string.

3 Reposition the head.
Place the head of the doll on the torso. You may need a second pair of hands to hold it steady while you prepare the string.

Insert the neck flange. Pull the strings tight and tie a knot above the flange to secure.

4. Pull the string to tighten.
Grasp the ends of the string and pull firmly until you feel it tighten around the neck flange and secure the head to the body.

5. Retie the string.
Tie the neck string in a square knot (see the diagram on page 49) to prevent it from coming loose. Tie a bow to shorten the ends of the string. Double-knot for added security.

HOW TO FIX A WAGON WHEEL

1 | Examine the wheel.

The wheel is generally held in place by two pins, one on either side of the hub, which is the center of the wheel. If the outer pin breaks, the wheel may fall off or become damaged. Most wagon wheel failures occur at the hub, which carries the weight of the wagon's load.

2 | Locate the wheel's bushing.

The center of the hub has a thin plastic or metal bushing—a $1/2$- to 1-inch section of tubing—that spins around the axle. Check for a missing or cracked bushing.

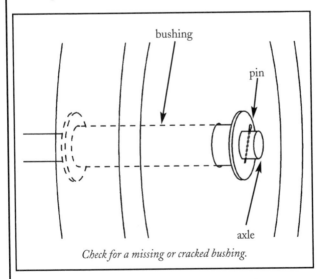

bushing

pin

axle

Check for a missing or cracked bushing.

3 Remove the bushing.

If the bushing is still present, use pliers to remove it. If the bushing has broken into several pieces, remove all pieces.

4 Construct a new bushing.

Cut a small section of plastic tubing—a section of garden hose or plastic pipe—to fit inside the wheel hub. (If the bushing is metal, use a hacksaw to cut a small section of metal pipe.) The new bushing should fit snugly inside the hub, but should be a few millimeters in diameter bigger than the axle so the wheel can spin freely. Use pliers or a rubber mallet to fit the bushing into the hub, if necessary.

5 Replace the wheel.

6 Spin the wheel.

The wheel should spin around the axle with no wobbling: If the wheel wobbles, the bushing is not tight against the hub and should be reseated.

7 Insert a bolt or pin through the axle.

Repair or replace the pins as necessary. If the pins are damaged and cannot be reused, insert small tacking nails through the pinholes. Bend the sharp end of the nail with a set of pliers to hold it in place. Be certain that the nails are secure and that there is no slippage.

How to Fix a Flat Bike Tire without a Patch

1 Release the brake.
Squeeze the brake, then pull out the brake cable from where it connects to the brake shoes next to the rim of the wheel.

2 Remove the wheel.
Open the quick-release lever or use a wrench to loosen the bolts from the wheel hub. Take the wheel off the bike.

3 Remove one side of the tire from the rim.
Insert the tip of a screwdriver, house key, or other metal instrument under the bead (the edge where the tire attaches to the rim) and press down on the tool. Repeat in several places until that side of the tire comes free.

4 Remove the tube.
Pull the tube out of the tire.

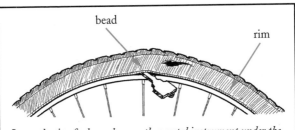

Insert the tip of a house key or other metal instrument under the bead to pry the tire from rim.

5 Construct an emergency patch.

Fold several small-denomination bills into squares or rectangles, depending on the size of the gash. Stack the folded bills and place the patch inside the tire. Cover the gash completely. If no cash is available, use a foil wrapper from an energy bar or candy bar.

6 Stuff the entire tire with leaves or grass.

Make sure your patch does not slip.

7 Replace the tire bead over the rim edge.

Use your hands to work the tire bead back over the rim edge. It may be necessary to use a key or screwdriver to fit the whole tire back on the rim. As you are working, you may need to add more grass or leaves to make the tire sturdy enough to ride. Once the tire is back on the rim, work both sides of the tire bead from side-to-side until it is fully secured.

8 Remount the wheel.

Replace the wheel by either snapping the quick-release lever back into position or by tightening the nuts that hold the wheel in place.

9 Ride home slowly.

Be Aware

A large gash in the tire's sidewall may result in the still-inflated tube sticking out of the tire. Serious injury may occur if the bike is ridden in this condition.

HOW TO REMOVE A HAND STUCK IN A JAR

1 Slather grease.
Spread cooking oil, butter, margarine, mayonnaise, or other greasy substance on the part of the hand that is accessible.

2 Try to slide out the hand.
Gently pull with steady, even pressure. Wedge the jar under your arm or have a third person hold the jar as you pull.

3 Submerge the hand and jar in ice water.
The combination of the greased hand and the cold, which reduces swelling, may release the hand.

4 Try to slide out the hand.

5 If the hand is still stuck, raise the hand.
Elevate the hand (and jar) above the level of the child's heart for five minutes to reduce swelling.

6 Try to slide out the hand.

7 Break the vacuum seal.
Slide a straw, eating utensil, or plastic tubing in between the hand and the edge of the jar. Do not use a knife with a sharp blade.

how to remove a hand stuck in a jar

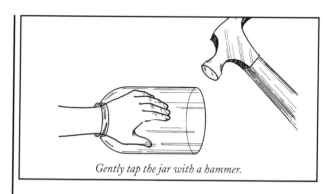
Gently tap the jar with a hammer.

8 Try to slide out the hand.

9 Break the jar.
If all else fails, shatter the jar by tapping with a hammer.
Tell the child to retract his hand to the opposite end.

10 Clear the debris.
Tell the child not to move his hand around until the task is finished and the hand is rinsed free of glass splinters.

How to Extract a Foot Stuck in Sinking Mud

1 Tell the child not to struggle and flail.
Calm the child and explain that she will not be swallowed up.

2 Instruct the child to let go of heavy objects.
Loaded backpacks, bags of gear, pockets filled with rocks, or other heavy items could drag her down farther.

3 Stabilize the surface around the hole and child.
Place planks, boards, or tree limbs on the ground so that you can approach the child. Use a walking stick, pole, or branch to test the ground's stability as you approach.

4 Grab the child and pull with steady upward momentum.
Approach the child from behind and grab the child's torso under the arms. Drag backwards. If her torso is not available for grabbing, pull the child by her hands, feet, or whatever is exposed.

How to Retrieve a Child Stuck in a Tree

1 Ask for directions.
Request that the child explain step by step how he got to where he is. This will focus his thoughts, calm him, and may provide a map as to how to climb back down.

2 Direct the descent.
From the ground, tell him where to put his hands and feet at each stage of the descent. Explain that if he was able to climb up, he should be able to climb back down.

3 Demonstrate how to climb down.
Select sturdy branches close to the ground and show him how to step on the part of the limb closest to the trunk.

Step close to the trunk.

Call for help.

4 Climb to his aid.

Grab a branch at its base and use your legs, not your arms, to power yourself up the tree. Make sure that three of your limbs are in contact with the tree at all times. Once you have reached your child, hold his hand and say soothing things to calm him.

5 Slowly talk your child down as you descend.

Your arms should bear your weight on the way down. To increase your grip on the branches during your descent, turn your palms toward you when gripping the branches. Do not carry your child down the tree.

6 Call for help.

If you both get stuck, shout to attract a passerby who can get help. If you have a mobile phone, call the fire department.

Be Aware

Do not allow a child to jump from the tree or try to catch a jumping child. If a 50-pound child jumps just 10 feet into your outstretched arms, he exerts about 300 pounds of force, enough to injure both of you on impact.

HOW TO RID A BEDROOM OF MONSTERS

1 Turn on the lights.
   Show your child that there are no monsters in the room.

2 Explain that you are making sure there will be no monsters in the future.

3 Spray infested areas with water.
   Monsters are afraid of water. Fill a spray bottle with water and lightly mist problem areas, including under the bed, around the door, and in the closet.

4 Place sentries outside of closets and by windows.
   Monsters will avoid friendly-looking stuffed animals, dolls, clowns, and puppets. Assemble a battalion of these around all likely points of entry.

5 Use the color green.
   Many monsters are afraid of the color green. Use a green night light or or encourage your child to wear pajamas with some green on them. A bandage, washable tattoo, nail polish, or a sticker with the color green are also effective.

Be Aware
If you encounter monsters, kill them with kindness. Hugs are particularly lethal, as are compliments.

HOW TO MAKE YOUR CHILD GET DRESSED

⭐ Offer a controlled choice.

Give your child two items to choose between so she will feel as though she is asserting herself. Ask, "This shirt or this shirt?" followed by "These pants or these pants?" Do not offer too many alternatives, and agree with whatever choice is made.

⭐ Wrap your child's clothes like a present.

Place your child's outfit in a box. Wrap the box in gaudy paper festooned with ribbons. Place the "present" at the foot of the child's bed so she gets up enthusiastically and finds her clothes all ready. The child may experience acute disappointment, however, when she discovers that she has not received a real present.

⭐ Play make-believe.

- Pretend your child is the local fire chief and must get dressed as quickly as possible to get to a fire.
- Pretend that your child has been selected to model clothes at a fashion show. Once dressed, she can parade back and forth on the "catwalk." Take a few photographs.

⭐ Race.

Race to complete dressing before your child. Allow her to win. Since she now understands the concept of speed-dressing, each day encourage her to race against her own times.

★ Distract.
Keep the child distracted by tickling, administering raspberries, or singing songs. Ask her to imitate animal sounds or recite the alphabet.

★ Warm the clothes.
In a dryer or on a radiator, warm the clothes you select and encourage your child to get dressed fast, while the clothes are still toasty warm.

★ Allow your child to wear pajamas to school.
Your child will quickly get the message that day clothes are preferable once she faces the stares of her peers.

Be Aware

- You're not done until the shoes are on, too. Make putting on shoes part of getting dressed or you will face a whole new struggle later.
- Offering a bribe—cash, extra television time, getting carried into the kitchen, dessert for breakfast—is inappropriate and sets a bad precedent. It can be extremely effective as a last resort, however (see "How to Bribe Your Child" on page 102).

HOW TO DEAL WITH A SMART ALECK

1 Ignore.
Children with easy-going temperaments will try out smart-aleck behavior once or twice and drop it if it doesn't get a response.

2 Alert your child to the offensive behavior.
If your child continues to display an impertinent attitude, point out specific information about his actions that are unacceptable. Raise a yellow flag, kept in your back pocket (the way a referee calls a foul), whenever your child says something obnoxious. Then give him a time-out.

3 Remove privileges.
Reduce access to favorite activities, such as watching television or playing outside, in accordance with the severity and frequency of the insolence. Clearly state the reason for the consequence. Place favorite toys or video games in a "toy prison," from which they can be paroled for the child's good behavior.

4 Do not sass back.
It will be tempting to respond in kind to offensive behavior; it is likely that you'd win a contest of wits, but you run the risk of encouraging your child to come up with better lines the next time.

5 Encourage your budding comedian.

Try to hone your child's wit into a marketable skill. Watch movies and listen to recordings featuring famous sarcastic comedians and work on his act. Beware that this could lead to the child becoming a "dirty talker," and, if the act succeeds, completely unmanageable.

Be Aware

Children learn to behave and speak by modeling what they observe at home. Do not use any language in front of the child that you would not want him repeating. Eliminate sarcasm, eye rolling, verbal mimicry, irony, and back talk from your own speech.

HOW TO MAKE YOUR CHILD EAT VEGETABLES

⭐ Eat vegetables yourself.
Be enthusiastic about vegetables. "Beans are awesome!" "Peas rule!" "Rutabagas rock!"

⭐ Talk in euphemisms.
Encourage your child by calling the vegetable a "growing food" or "brain food" or "run-fast food" or "beauty food."

⭐ Require one bite.
Even if she does not like it, with the "one-bite rule" the child should eventually grow accustomed to the taste, though it may take years.

⭐ Let the child select the vegetable.
Take your child to the grocery store to pick out one vegetable. Invite her into the kitchen to help you prepare it for dinner. She will become emotionally invested in the vegetable and proud of it. She may not only eat the vegetable, she may urge others to do so.

⭐ Sneak vegetables into other dishes.
Camouflage vegetables in stews, lasagna, pot pies, pizza toppings, casseroles, or soups.

Arrange vegetables in unusual ways.

⭐ Change presentation.
Arrange vegetables in a happy face. Use unnaturally
colored ketchup (pink, green, blue) to jazz up a pile of
vegetables. Make trees with broccoli and asparagus,
boats from endive, and a lake out of guacamole.

⭐ Prepare the vegetable in different ways.
If she rejected the steamed broccoli, next time serve it
raw with a dip. If the asparagus in cream sauce was
not popular, try it with butter and lemon. Use a
blender or a juicer to transform the vegetable into a
purée or a smoothie.

Make vegetables the only option.

Designate "vegetarian night" and serve nothing but vegetables. Your child will eat them if she is hungry and there is no other food available. When the meal is over, declare the kitchen closed and do not allow snacks or dessert.

 Do not make food into a battle of wills.

Be matter-of-fact about whether your child does or does not eat her vegetables. Do not force a vegetable on your child or bribe her to eat. Do not say, "If you eat your brussels sprouts, you can have dessert." This will interfere with her developing a genuine affection for the vegetable, and reinforce sweets as the truly desirable food.

HOW TO BRIBE YOUR CHILD

1 Make an offer you know your child can't refuse.
Offer what your child desires most—money, new CDs, more video game time, candy.

2 Do not offer too much initially.
If you are willing to give your child a quarter every time he remembers to flush the toilet, start lower—offer a dime first, and expect a couple rounds of negotiation. Children today are savvy negotiators.

3 Get performance first, then pay.
Withhold payment until you have determined that your child has carried out the other side of the bargain. Children often conveniently forget their promises.

IF YOU WISH TO CONCEAL THE BRIBE

1 Make certain that you are alone when discussing terms.
Even younger siblings who you think do not understand can turn you in.

2 Arrange a "dead drop" for making payments.
Select a location in or around the home where you will deposit the bribe. Place the item(s) in a gym bag or another commonly seen container. Leave the bag at the predetermined spot (in the laundry basket, behind

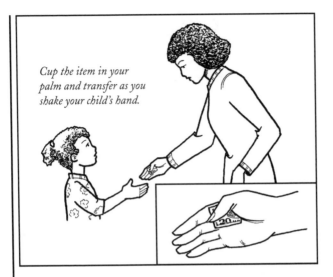

Cup the item in your palm and transfer as you shake your child's hand.

the coats in the closet, under your child's bed) and walk away quickly.

3 Master the "magician's palm" technique when paying with coins or bills.

Hold the item in your palm, cupping it slightly. Congratulate your child on "a job well done" or on his maturity. Shake your child's hand, and give him the money.

Be Aware

- Bribes are highly effective but are almost always an indication of weak or lazy parenting. Choose what is most important at that moment.
- Couples frequently disagree over whether to bribe children. Children almost always are in favor of it.

HOW TO SURVIVE A LONG CAR TRIP

1 Line the seats with a large bath towel or sheet.
The cover will protect the back seat and expedite cleanup later.

2 Leave early.
Start a long trip early—before dawn—to assure that kids will be sleepy and will nap for the first few hours of the ride. If they awaken at or near rush hour, pull over to avoid traffic and get a break from driving.

Bring only what you really need.

3 Bring along a few key items, but only what you really need.

Essential items include snacks, games, open-ended creative toys, and passive entertainment devices (such as CD players and portable DVD players).

4 Make frequent stops.

Do not expect small children to sit still for more than an hour or two at a time. Make frequent rest stops to switch drivers, stretch, throw a ball, run around, and use the bathroom. These stops also serve to fend off carsickness and keep the driver alert.

How to Pee at the Side of the Road

1 Pull over.

Find a spot with adequate coverage, usually in the form of bushes or thick trees, that is a safe distance from the road.

2 Exit the car away from the road.

Leave the door open to further block visibility. Take tissues or napkins with you, if available.

3 Select a position behind a tree or bush.

Position your child 180 degrees from view of oncoming traffic. In general, boys should pee facing downhill, while girls should pee facing uphill.

4 Assess the weather conditions.

Assess the direction of the wind, and position your child to pee with it.

5 Assemble a "human shield."

If there is little or no coverage, line up other members of the family to form a "human shield."

6 Keep quiet.

Do not speak to the family member who is attempting to go. It may be distracting and will only prolong the stop and the trip.

child answering nature's call

HOW TO SURVIVE PLAYING CATCH

1 Eat right.
Start the day with a high-protein, high-carbohydrate breakfast: Pancakes and sausage, bacon and eggs, or a bagel and an egg are all good choices. Drink plenty of fluids to aid in digestion, but avoid excess caffeine, which dehydrates. Wait 30 to 45 minutes for the meal to digest before playing ball.

2 Stretch.
Get the blood flowing with 15 to 20 minutes of intense stretching, fast jumping jacks, and vigorous running in place (get your knees up high). Make sure all major muscle groups—especially your arms, shoulders, thighs, and upper and lower back—are loose.

3 Tape ankles.
Wrap your ankles in first-aid tape to add support and reduce the chance of a twist or sprain.

4 Don head- and wristbands.
Keep sweat out of your eyes and off your hands.

5 Wear protective eyewear.
You may be forced to shag some flies or grab some pop-ups. Sunglasses will reduce glare and eyestrain and make the ball more visible. Wear a hat for added protection from the sun.

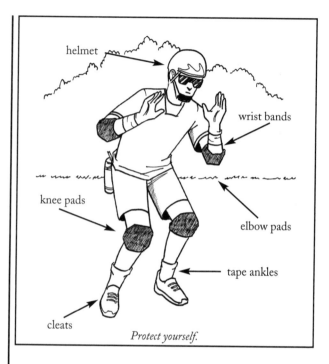

helmet

wrist bands

knee pads

elbow pads

tape ankles

cleats

Protect yourself.

6 Wear knee and elbow pads.
Pads will protect your joints should you need to dive, slide, or roll, or should you trip.

7 Wear cleats.
Cleats provide added traction.

8 Play ball.

HOW TO SURVIVE A SOCCER SATURDAY

★ Stay positive.
Refrain from criticizing your child's gameplay or the skills of the other children. Shout only supportive comments, such as "Good header" or "Nice shot." Lead the other parents in group cheers.

★ Focus on the game.
Do not gossip with the other parents or talk on your cell phone.

★ Do not criticize your child's coach.
Don't worry about how much playing time your child gets or criticize the coach's strategy.

★ Let the referee make the calls.
Refrain from yelling "Offside" and "Hand ball!" Support the referee no matter what calls he makes.

★ Bring healthful treats.
Fruit or trail mix makes the best refreshment for tired players, siblings, and parents. Bring a cooler with sports drinks, including water.

★ Bring folding chairs and extra clothing.
"Camp" folding chairs are appropriate but chaise longues are not. In sunny weather, pack hats and sun block. In cold weather, bring blankets and extra jackets.

how to survive a soccer saturday

Be Aware

- Know the rules: A player is "offside" (not "off-sides") when she is nearer to the other team's goal line than two of the opposing players and when the ball touches or is played by one of her team-mates. For determining an offside penalty, the ball counts as a "player" on the opposing team. The rule prevents players from hanging around the other team's goal. The consequence for a player being caught offside is the loss of possession.

- To cut down on annoying chatter, bring lollipops, jawbreakers, or other candy that takes a long time to dissolve. Pass them out to fans of both the home and away team. The visiting team will be impressed by your team's friendliness and may conduct themselves in a more civil manner. In any event, everyone's mouth will be occupied.

How to Break Up a Fight

1 Talk the parents down.
Do not yell; speak in a low, even tone and show understanding. Instruct the fighting parents to cease and desist. Call them by name, if you know their names. Remind the parents that they are setting a bad example for their children.

2 Prepare to intercede.
If the parents continue to fight, enlist the aid of another, preferably large, parent. Take off glasses, jewelry, or high heels. Disperse any audience that has

Separate the fighting parents.

Use water bottles to distract the fighters.

how to survive a soccer saturday

gathered. The fighters may feel a need to continue or save face if they are in front of a crowd.

3 Step between the fighting parents.
Position yourself in the middle of the fray. Extend your arms straight out to either side to push the parents as far from each other as possible. Continue to speak to the fighters in a calm but firm voice.

4 If you are with another person, pull the parents off of each other from behind.
From behind, clutch one of the sparring parents in a strong bear hug. Position your body with your chest pressing against his back. Reach your arms around him, over top of his arms, and grasp your hands together on his chest. Your partner should do the same with the other parent. Drag the opponents away from each other. Do not lift the parents off the ground: You will be susceptible to flailing legs and kicks to the shins, as well as to back strain.

5 Take fighters to separate areas.
Remove the parents to opposite sides of the field, or escort one of them to the parking lot, until you are assured that they have calmed down enough to finish watching the game in peace.

Be Aware

To break up a fight from a distance:

- Throw the contents of a large cooler on the fighting parents, or use squirt bottles to direct streams of water at their faces.
- Blow air horns near the fighters to frighten them.
- Throw slippery halftime snacks, like oranges, apples, or banana peels, under their feet to destabilize the fighting surface.
- Toss blankets or large towels over the heads of the fighters to disorient them.
- Pelt the fighters with soccer balls to distract them.

HOW TO TREAT A BLACK EYE

1 Make a cold compress.
Fill a clean sock with ice from the snack cooler. A cold can of soda or a juice box will also work.

2 Sit down.
Sit on a folding chair or on the ground.

3 Tilt your head back.
With your head tilted back, gravity will aid in reducing the swelling. Angle your head so that you can still watch the game with your good eye.

4 Cover the injured eye with the compress.
Use minimal pressure. If the compress is too cold, use a thicker cloth. Keep the compress over your eye for at least an hour or for the rest of the game.

HOW TO SURVIVE WHEN YOUR CHILD BRINGS HOME A STRAY

Dog

1 Involve your child in finding the dog's owner.
Explain that the dog might be somebody else's pet.
Ask her to make posters to put up around the neighborhood. Call the local humane society to determine if the pet has been reported missing. Have her speak to the local mail carrier and other dog owners in the area who might recognize the dog.

2 Check the dog's tags.
A dog kept as a pet should have a rabies tag, and may have a name tag. Contact animal control authorities, who can use the rabies ID number to locate the animal's vet and owner.

3 Follow the dog.
Take the dog back to the place where it was found and encourage the dog to lead you and your child to its home. Put the dog on a leash. Repeat, "Go home, boy!" or "Dinner time!" to motivate the dog. If you live in an area where several languages are spoken, repeat these phrases in each language.

4 Take the dog to a veterinarian.

The vet should give the dog a full behavioral and medical evaluation. The dog's mental and physical condition may determine whether it can be a suitable pet.

5 Discuss dog ownership responsibilities.

Explain to the child that caring for a dog is hard work. Detail pet care duties, and create a contract to make sure your child is fully vested in caring for and loving your new dog.

Be Aware

A dog with a runny nose, badly matted hair, and a dirty or unkempt appearance may have been on the streets for weeks or longer—approach such a dog with caution. Be wary of a dog that drinks lots of water and seems confused, withdrawn, or aggressive. Never approach any dog that appears to be foaming at the mouth.

Exchange Student

1 Involve your child in finding the student's origins.

Explain to your child that the student may already have a host family. "Found" signs should be created and posted around the local high school, college, or university.

2 Check the student's papers.

An exchange student should have a valid passport and student visa, and usually a letter of introduction to the school. School authorities should be able to reach the student's parents to verify his status.

how to survive when your child brings home a stray

3 Follow the student.

Take the student back to the place where he was found and encourage him to lead you and your child to his host family. Repeat, "Take me to your host family," or "Show me where you live." If the student smiles and nods but does not follow your instructions, repeat these phrases in several languages until the student responds appropriately.

4 Take the student to a health clinic.

The doctor should give the student a full medical and behavioral evaluation.

5 Discuss moving-in responsibilities, and prepare for a long stay.

While exchange students are generally friendly once they feel comfortable in their new surroundings, they can overstay their welcomes. Give the student his own bedroom, if available, and access to soft drinks, a television, and a telephone. (Be prepared for expensive long-distance telephone calls.)

Be Aware

Observe the student's condition and behavior. A student with a runny nose, badly matted hair, and a dirty or unkempt appearance may have been on the streets for weeks or longer—approach such a student with caution. Be wary of a student who drinks constantly and seems confused, withdrawn, or aggressive. Never approach any student who appears to be foaming at the mouth.

HOW TO DEAL WITH A DEAD PET

1 Make sure the pet is really dead.

Cats often sleep without moving for hours, dogs can be lazy, reptiles are cold blooded and still, fish with parasites sometimes float upside down at the surface, and opossums are well known for feigning. Observe the pet's chest: If it rises and falls, even very slowly, the animal is still alive. Hold a mirror to the pet's nose. If no condensation appears, the animal is probably dead. Pick up the animal. If it does not move and its body is stiff and cold, it has passed away. Feel the neck for a pulse. If you cannot feel one, and all the other signs indicate death, the pet has died. Finally, check for involuntary blinking reflex: Lightly touch the pet's cornea. Any animal that is alive will blink reflexively.

2 Break the news to your child.

If the pet's death was sudden and unexpected, the child is likely to be distraught. Explain that death is a fact of life. Emphasize that the pet had a happy life, the child had taken good care of it, and that the pet is not suffering.

3 Prepare the body.

Close the animal's eyelids—you may need to hold them in place for several seconds so they will stay closed. Place the corpse in a matchbox, shoe box, or wooden box and cover with a washcloth, towel, or sheet, depending on the size of the pet.

4 Hold a family funeral.
Pets are a part of the family, and children expect them to be buried when they die. Give everyone a chance to speak at the funeral ceremony. Burial should immediately follow the ceremony, though there may be laws restricting the burial of pets in a yard. Check with your local vet on burial options, or contact a pet cemetery.

5 Allow your child to grieve.
Do not replace the pet right away. Grieving is an important part of the recovery process, and children should be given time to adapt to the loss.

Be Aware

- A pet cemetery charges from $100 to many thousands of dollars, depending on the coffin, type of service, and size and quality of the headstone/plaque.
- Many vets have cremation services available. If the local vet cannot help with disposal, the local public health department or any large veterinary hospital or university will have facilities.

HOW TO SURVIVE A SLUMBER PARTY

1 Begin the party at around 6 P.M.
Organize strenuous events such as tag, soccer, high-impact aerobics, calisthenics, or wind-sprint drills to exhaust the guests and encourage an early bedtime.

2 Serve carbohydrate-heavy foods.
Pizza, pasta, sandwiches, chili, and other heavy foods help induce sleep. Make certain these are on the menu, and encourage everyone to go back for seconds.

Calisthenics will encourage an early bedtime.

3 Secure cabinets, rooms, and drawers you want to keep off limits.

Use travel padlocks and cable ties to protect cabinets and drawers. To keep the children out of rooms that do not lock, place noisy pets inside the rooms, or stack cans behind the door to create an "intruder alert" system.

4 Observe your guests unobtrusively.

Use small bowls for snacks so they need to be refilled regularly, providing you with the opportunity to ensure that the children are behaving well. Listen with a tall glass pressed against a wall or door (holding the closed end to your ear) to eavesdrop. Check in every half an hour or so in order to "see if anyone needs or wants anything."

5 Introduce video games and movies to ratchet down the activity level.

Lower energy levels with nonviolent video games as part of a cool-down phase. Show long, sweeping epic movies around 11 P.M. to get children into sleeping bags and a prone position.

Be Aware

When issuing invitations to the party, advise your guests to bring not only sleeping bags, pillows, and toothbrushes, but also their favorite board games, video games, game controllers, and stuffed animals.

CHAPTER 3

THE TEENAGE YEARS

HOW TO TELL IF YOUR CHILD WAS SWITCHED AT BIRTH

1 Compare a photograph of yourself or your spouse as teenagers to a photograph of your child.

Look particularly at facial features—eyes, nose, mouth—and at body shape. If there are absolutely no similarities and your child was not adopted, you might be right: This strangely behaving person may not be your biological child. Proceed to step 2.

2 Compare personality traits.

Look for common tendencies and habits that are signs of a genetic connection. Allow for generation-specific differences such as musical taste and fashion sense.

3 Examine what happened immediately after your child's birth.

- Did you actually see the doctor place the ID band on your child's arm or leg in the hospital room?
- Was your child out of your immediate view for more than a few seconds?
- Did you notice any marked similarities between yourself and any other children in the nursery?

If the answer to any of the above questions is "yes" or "I don't know," look for further evidence of a long-ago error.

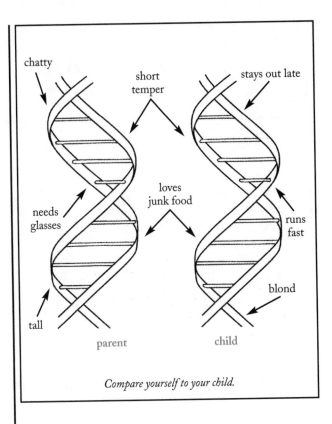

chatty

short
temper

stays out late

needs
glasses

loves
junk food

runs
fast

tall

blond

parent

child

Compare yourself to your child.

Be Aware
- Your child's difficult and dissimilar traits might be attributable to your spouse.
- DNA testing is expensive, and by now you're a family anyway.

how to tell if your child was switched at birth

HOW TO SOUNDPROOF YOUR TEENAGER'S ROOM

1 Move speakers away from walls.
Speakers placed directly against a wall will reverberate sound through the wall and into adjoining rooms. Also raise the speakers off the floor and place them on stands or small tables to reduce reverberations through the floor.

2 Lower the volume.
Turn down the volume 30 percent, then move the speakers closer to your teenager to provide him with the same volume of sound.

3 Disable bass-boosting features.
Bass-enhanced sound travels through most partitions more easily. Turn off the feature on the amplifier or equalizer.

4 Install carpeting.
A thick carpet with a rubber pad below it will absorb most sounds. Make sure it runs wall to wall. Do not hang carpeting or rugs on the walls. Soft, absorbent materials applied to walls change the acoustics of a room but rarely make it more soundproof.

Encourage your child to use headphones.

5 Install a solid wood door.

Solid wood doors offer better soundproofing than hollow-core or recessed-panel doors.

6 Install weather stripping.

Sound "leaks" from a room through the space around the door. Add sponge rubber weather stripping seals on the top, bottom, and sides of all doors.

Be Aware

Studio-quality headphones make an excellent present for your teenager. Explain that they enhance the quality of the sound and can really be blasted; hope that headphones replace the speakers.

HOW TO COPE WITH YOUR TEENAGER'S MUSICAL PREFERENCES

⭐ Buy yourself earplugs.

⭐ Create loud white noise.
Run the vacuum or turn on a wave machine set at the tsunami level to relax when your teen turns on his music.

⭐ Learn to be "down" with your teen's music.
It will weird him out and probably make him switch his preferences. Eagerly ask if he has the latest [*insert his favorite music group*] disc. Proudly show off the poster, T-shirt, and other memorabilia you have collected of said group. Sing along whenever he plays the group's CDs.

⭐ Dig up embarrassing "early years" information on your teen's favorite group.
Find humiliating photographs of the band when it was starting out. You are bound to come across lame hair and clothing styles. Reveal damning facts on the band such as any classical training, experiences with all-boy or all-girl bands, and appearances on network television talent-search programs.

⭐ Say you heard the creepy neighbor's preteen listening to the same music last week.

HOW TO DEAL WITH PROVOCATIVE CLOTHING

1 In a firm and calm voice, tell your teen to change into something more suitable.

Do not yield to a tantrum. Remain neutral and impervious to eye rolling and heavy sighs.

2 In a calm and firm voice, tell your teen to change into something more suitable.

Do not yield to a tantrum. Remain neutral and impervious to eye rolling and heavy sighs.

3 In a firm and calm voice, tell your teen to change into something more suitable.

Do not yield a to tantrum. Remain neutral and impervious to eye rolling and heavy sighs.

4 In a calm and firm voice, tell your teen to change into something more suitable.

Do not yield to a tantrum. Remain neutral and impervious to eye rolling and heavy sighs.

5 Employ reverse psychology.

Wear the same outfit as your teen. The anarchy T-shirt, hoodie sweatshirt with silk-screened profanity, or teeny tiny skirt and ripped fishnet stockings will not look as cool when you are wearing them, too.

HOW TO BOND WITH YOUR TEENAGER

Perform an Ollie on a Skateboard

1 Position your feet on the board.
Place your non-dominant foot toward the front of the deck (the wooden part of the board) over the trucks (front axle). Place the foot at a comfortable angle, not quite forward and not completely to the side. Angle your dominant foot across the board at the tail (rear end) of the board.

2 Bend your knees.
Your knees should be slightly bent to help you keep your balance.

3 Propel the board slowly forward.
Remove your back foot from the deck and use it to push on the ground and propel the board forward. Once it begins rolling, put your foot back in place at the rear of the board.

4 Slide your front foot back.
Move your front foot back about six inches, toward the middle of the deck.

Kick down hard on the tail of the deck.
The front of the board will rise off the ground.

Land.

how to bond with your teenager

5 Kick the tail down.

Kick down hard on the tail section of the deck, while at the same time lifting your front foot up and springing up off your back foot. The front of the board will rise off the ground.

6 Move your front foot forward.

With the front of the board still in the air, move your front foot forward slightly while airborne. This will raise the tail section and get the skateboard completely off the ground. You may find it easier to simply rotate your front ankle, so the board is pivoting on the outside edge of your leading foot.

7 Stay centered over the deck.

While floating in midair, keep your feet centered over the board, since you will need to be properly positioned to land. Both you and the skateboard will be traveling forward at the same rate of speed, so this is a natural movement.

8 Let gravity take the board back.

The board will land with the wheels down, since the wheels and axles are heavier than the deck.

9 Land on the board.

Bend your knees to help absorb the impact of the landing.

DJ a Party

1 Spin the first record.

Select a song with a strong intro to establish the tone for the rest of the set. Place the first record on the left deck (or record player). Move the crossfader all the way to the left, so that channel will play the music. The left deck corresponds with channel one, the right deck corresponds with channel two.

2 Drop the needle.

Put the needle down on your record to play the song for the crowd.

3 Plug in the headphones.

The mixer has a cue input, or a $1/4$-inch jack for headphones, that allows you to hear what's coming up next without broadcasting the music over the speakers.

4 Cue up a song.

Select the next track to blend with the song that is now playing through the speakers. Put the new track on the right deck, which will play on channel two, and make sure that the cue is set to play channel two. Hold one headphone to your ear, leaving your other ear free to hear the music playing to the house and to gauge the crowd reaction.

5 Line up eight counts.

Count from one to eight in time with the beats (or bass drum hits) of the song playing over the speaker.

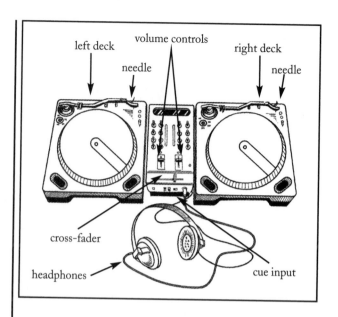

left deck   volume controls   right deck

needle   needle

cross-fader

headphones   cue input

Play the cue song over your headphones, and line up the eight counts so the "1s" match. Use your finger to slow down or start the record on channel two to match the beats.

6 Cross fade into the new track.
The cross-fader is a rectangular slider control located at the bottom of the mixer. It slides horizontally rather than vertically, like the volume controls. Use the cross fader to blend the two channels.

7 Maintain song continuity.
Mixing the two songs at the right place is critical to keeping the crowd involved and dancing. Most dance

songs and DJ remixes have breaks, or areas of the song where the vocals and music purposely drop out and give you a chance to beat mix. Avoid mixing into or out of a track during a vocal segment.

8 Watch the crowd.

The crowd is the best gauge of how well you are DJing. If people are having fun—and, especially, if they are easily dancing through the transitions between songs—you are doing a good job. If, on the other hand, they are having trouble dancing to the beat, alter your song selections.

Be Aware

- Every mixer is different. Familiarize yourself with the equipment in the booth.

- Using a stopwatch or a watch or clock with a second hand, count the beats of the current song (or bass drum hits) for 15 seconds, then multiply by four to determine the number of beats per minute (BPM). Most sets begin with songs with a lower BPM, then gradually increase the BPM as the music increases in intensity. As a general rule, consider 88 to 110 BPM for a hip hop or rap music set, and 116 to 140 BPM for a house/techno set.

- Do not play the new song at a lower volume after the fade in. The volumes of the two songs should match, since a lower volume diminishes a song's energy.

how to bond with your teenager

HOW TO SURVIVE TEENAGE ANGST

 The Dark Poet

TELLTALE SIGNS: Black clothes, dark lipstick or nail polish, beret, cape of any color, carries book at all times, sullen, avoids direct sunlight.

WHAT HE/SHE WANTS: New family (suspects switched at birth), castle on a stormy heath, fangs, to write own zine.

WHAT TO SAY: "What a lovely moon tonight."

WHAT TO GIVE: *The Collected Works of Edgar Allan Poe.*

 The Spaz

TELLTALE SIGNS: Bumps into people and things, nervous tics, resembles overgrown puppy, tape on glasses, menace on the dance floor.

WHAT HE/SHE WANTS: Coordination, timing, to make the winning shot, cancellation of gym class.

WHAT TO SAY: "Don't worry, it will heal fast."

WHAT TO GIVE: Helmet, kneepads.

 The Lovelorn

TELLTALE SIGNS: Flavored lip gloss, body glitter, furtive glances, seductive gait, nervous laughter, serial crushes.

WHAT HE/SHE WANTS: First kiss, boyfriend/girlfriend, to wear his/her Varsity jacket, someone to linger at locker with, recipient for reams of love poetry.

WHAT TO SAY: "I didn't go to my prom either."
WHAT TO GIVE: Puppy.

⭐ The Rebel

TELLTALE SIGNS: Black leather or red canvas jacket, white T-shirts with smokes rolled up in sleeve, belligerent, curt, squinty.

WHAT HE/SHE WANTS: To be freed from the shackles of oppression, parent to sweat over threats to move out, love and affection, boundaries, warm milk, cat to sleep on pillow.

WHAT TO SAY: "If nothing matters, why not enjoy?"
WHAT TO GIVE: Cool jeans.

⭐ The Loner

TELLTALE SIGNS: Stands near walls or in corners, travels solo by choice, slinks around house and school, headphones, heavy book bag, big sunglasses.

WHAT HE/SHE WANTS: Privacy, solitude, time for reading and thinking, an end to prying stares, flat screen TV, year off to meditate.

WHAT TO SAY: Nothing.
WHAT TO GIVE: Isolation tank.

⭐ The Egotist

TELLTALE SIGNS: Satisfied smirk, knows most everything, pained at having to listen to and make conversation at dinner table, coordinated separates, booming voice, eye rolling, heavy sighs, excellent grooming habits.

What he/she wants: Recognition, confirmation, validation, vindication, personal assistant.
What to say: "That's nice, dear."
What to give: Monocle.

⭐ The Worry Wart
Telltale signs: Wringing of hands, nail biting, furrowed brow, downcast glances, makes lots of lists.
What he/she wants: End to contingency planning, someone else to take charge, early acceptance into college of choice, fun.
What to say: "In the long run, it will all be okay."
What to give: Worry beads.

⭐ The Looks Police
Telltale signs: Relentless self-scrutiny, armed with fashion magazines, water bottle and gym bag, avoids salad dressing.
What he/she wants: Clear dewy skin, to be "discovered," to lose 20 pounds, to be leggy, boobs (if female), to lose boobs (if male), six-pack abs, good hair, admiring glances.
What to say: "You look great!"
What to give: Magnifying mirror.

HOW TO SURVIVE YOUR CHILD'S FIRST DATE

1 Meditate.

A few hours before the date, exercise, practice yoga or tai chi, or meditate. Take deep breaths in through your nose and out through your mouth. Listen to soothing music. If you take an anti-anxiety medication, make sure that you do not miss a dose that day. Alternatively, consume one cocktail 30 to 45 minutes before the date is scheduled to begin.

2 Lay the ground rules.

Inform your teen that you have a few simple requirements before she leaves on her date:

- Completion of a "dating plan" before departure, including the name of the date, age, and contact information, the intended venues and activities for the date, the names and contact information for other participants, and approximate time frame.
- Approval of attire, including amount of skin visible, number of tears in clothes, color and style of hair, makeup, and jewelry.
- Date must come inside to pick up her up. Honking or calling via cell phone when outside the house is not acceptable.
- Ask now any questions she has about the "Birds and the Bees" (see page 162).

If the date does not meet your gaze and withdraws his hand quickly, you know you are in control.

- Curfews must be adhered to.
- Promise to call for any reason, including having a bad time, want a ride home, will be late—but can't be late.

3 Shake hands with the date.

Greet him with an unnecessarily long, firm handshake and good eye contact. If the date looks away and attempts to withdraw his hand quickly, this is a positive sign—you are making him uncomfortable; you are in control. If the date attempts to overpower your handshake and meets your gaze with a steely glare, he is challenging you and you should be worried.

4 Assess the date's attire.

Dressing too provocatively or too conservatively means the date is working too hard on his image.

5 Assess the date's age.

Excess facial or gray hair, crow's feet, and telltale phrases such as "when I was your age," "back in the day," and "they don't make them like they used to" are signs that your teen's date is no longer a teen himself.

6 Remind yourself that dating is a rite of passage, that you survived, and that your teen will, too.

GAMES TO PLAY WHILE WAITING UP

⭐ Guess the arrival time.

Each parent guesses the exact arrival time of the teen (hour and minute). As the chosen times pass with no arrival, each parent picks a new time. The parent with the time closest to the actual arrival wins.

⭐ Pick the excuse.

Each parent chooses three excuses the teen may use upon late arrival. The parent with the right excuse is the winner.

⭐ Name the commercial.

Turn on the television. The first person to correctly pick the name of the product being advertised— before it is mentioned—wins.

Be Aware

- Do not talk too long with the date. Five minutes of polite conversation is adequate when meeting the date. Do not show home movies or flip through photo albums. Do not take the date's picture or attempt to videotape the first date.
- Give your child a watch that is set ten minutes fast.
- Avoid direct interrogation. Do not say, "So, what are your intentions with my daughter?"
- Do not tag along on your child's first date. If you must see what goes on, follow from at least three or four cars back.

Direct Question:	Tactful Question:
How old are you?	Who did you vote for in the last election? The one before that?
Do you smoke?	Want a smoke?
Are you an alcoholic?	Want a drink?
Do you do drugs?	Are you holding?
What are your intentions?	Will I be seeing you again?

HOW TO SURVIVE YOUR CHILD'S FIRST DRIVING LESSON

1 Dress casually.
Do not wear a helmet or extra padding.

2 Check safety devices.
Make sure seatbelts are securely fastened and mirrors are properly adjusted.

3 Breathe in deeply and exhale slowly.
Continue to breathe.

4 Relax.
Do not tense your muscles.

5 Keep your hands folded in front of you.

6 Avoid sudden movements.
Do not clench the dashboard, grab for the emergency brake handle, or make other movements that may surprise the teen and cause him to lose control. Do not smoke, eat, read, sing, play the radio, finger worry beads, or talk on the telephone.

Relax. It will be fine.

7 Compliment the driving.
Avoid the urge to comment negatively on your child's performance. Do not say things like "You're going to get us both killed!" Speak positively and in a calm voice.

8 Do not grab the steering wheel, gear shift, or hand brake.
Trust the driver.

9 Stay relaxed.
It will be fine.

How to Reattach a Damaged Bumper

1 Assess the damage.

Examine the bumper and bumper cover. Many vehicles have a plastic or rubber bumper cover over a steel bumper. The lightweight cover, rather than the steel bumper, is likely to be the damaged portion.

2 Remove the bumper cover.

If the cover is completely separated from the bumper, reattachment is not advisable. Place bumper cover in the trunk or backseat and seek professional repair. If the cover is only partially separated from the car, proceed to step 3.

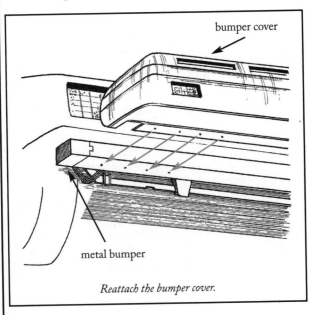

bumper cover

metal bumper

Reattach the bumper cover.

3 Check bumper cover bolts.

Bumper covers on passenger cars are attached in four to six places, generally with plastic screws or metal bolts through the bumper cover and into the plastic or metal bumper itself. Examine screw or bolt holes to determine if they have been ripped or are still usable.

4 Reattach bumper cover with wire.

If the holes are still intact, tie bumper back on the bumper frame with wire, string, rope, or yarn. Feed the wire through the holes where the bumper cover has come loose. Make several passes through the holes for security. Tie with square knots (see diagram on page 49).

5 Reattach bumper cover with duct tape.

If the mounting holes have been ripped or are inaccessible, apply duct tape completely around the bumper and cover. If necessary, tape the bumper cover to the hood of the car to prevent slippage.

Be Aware

- Plan the driving route so that you are able to return home via public transportation, if necessary.
- Car bumpers, as opposed to bumper covers, are very heavy, and damage to the bumper itself may be indicative of more serious damage to the radiator, shock absorbers, or the steel in the wheel wells. If you notice liquid leaking out from the engine area, call for a tow.

HOW TO TRACK YOUR TEENAGER'S MOVEMENTS

HOW TO DETERMINE IF YOUR CHILD IS DRIVING YOUR CAR

1 Purchase an inexpensive, analog watch.

2 Place the watch behind a rear tire of your car.
Place the watch before you go to bed at night or away on a trip. If your car is not parked so that it has to be backed up to be moved, place another watch in front of a front tire.

3 Check the watch.
In the morning or on your return, examine the watch. If your child has taken the car while you were away, it will have been crushed, stopping the machinery at the exact time and date.

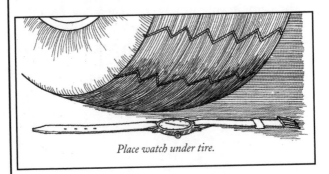

Place watch under tire.

How to Determine If Your Child Is Sneaking Out at Night

1 After your child goes to his room for bed, remove a hair from your head.

2 Attach the hair to the door of your child's room.
Use saliva to place one end of the hair on the door-frame and the other on the door itself.

3 Wake up earlier than your child in the morning.

4 Check for the hair.
If your child has left the room during the night, the hair will have become detached or fallen off.

Be Aware
- If your teenager's room has a window to the garden, water the garden thoroughly each night and rake the dirt smooth. Look for footprints in the morning.
- If you do not have enough hair for the door-hair alarm, if your teen needs to open the door to go to the bathroom, or if a pet might dislodge the hair, grease the front door knob with butter. Check in the morning to see if the knob has been wiped clean so it could be turned and the door opened.

HOW TO SURVIVE A MEETING WITH THE PRINCIPAL

1 | Dress appropriately.

Dress neatly and conservatively: a dark suit and solid or wide-striped tie for men, a dark suit or a dark skirt and neutral color blouse for women. Shoes should be clean, with laces tied. The principal is likely to make judgments about your parenting skills (and your child's behavior) based on your appearance.

2 | Use proper salutations.

If you know you are in the right, call the principal "Principal" followed by her last name. Using the title will appear to show respect; you are not challenging her authority, you just happen to be in the right. If you are in the wrong, do not mention the title when addressing her. Call her "Miss" or "Ms.," which levels the playing field.

3 | Observe the principal's reaction to meeting you.

If the principal comes around her desk and sits near you, this is a sign that the meeting is not likely to be confrontational. If the principal takes her place behind a desk, suggest moving the meeting to a more "comfortable" site, away from her home turf, such as a faculty break room, cafeteria, or a nearby coffee shop.

4 | Mirror the principal's body language.

If the principal leans to the right and cocks her head to the right, lean left and cock your head to the left. Mirroring nonverbal behavior—also called matching and pacing—is an effective way to put another person at ease and make them more amenable to suggestion. Avoid crossing your arms, which connotes defensiveness.

5 | Keep your story short and to the point.

The principal may try to interview you and your child separately, turning one against the other. Confer with your child before the meeting to get his side of the case. Make sure your claims and excuses are consistent and brief. The longer the justification or explanation, the more guilty you seem, and the more likely you are to contradict yourself or your child.

6 | Take notes.

Make sure the principal notices you are keeping a written record of the conversation. This conveys that you are a serious and conscientious person. Do not tape-record the meeting, however, since the machine will create a barrier, defensiveness, and formality, at the same time that it implies you will lose and need the tape later.

7 | Ask open-ended questions.

Questions that begin with words like "what," "how," "why," "could," and "would" encourage the principal to offer longer, more expository answers, which serve to give you more information about the situation. Avoid asking questions prefaced with words like "do," "did," "is," and "are," which encourage shorter answers, and call for conclusions that might put you on the defensive.

8 When you get the answer you want, move on.
If the principal agrees with you on a point, don't rehash it or continue down the same path; switch to a new topic. Later, you can use any information gained to your advantage: "But didn't you say a few minutes ago that she's an excellent student?"

9 Concede meaningless points.
Do not admit to anything major, but make the principal think you are on her side by agreeing to tangential arguments. Say, "Yes, you are right, my son is bigger and stronger than most of the other children in his class."

10 Create the impression you're all on the same side.
Do not make the meeting seem adversarial: You, your child, and the principal are trying to solve a common problem. If necessary, create understanding and a shared-problem bond with the principal and distance yourself from your child, or from children in general. ("Kids will be kids.") If the principal has a rapport with you and trusts you to supervise your child, your child is more likely to get off easy.

Be Aware
Even if you feel your child has been wrongfully accused, fighting the principal may be a losing battle—and you don't want to make things worse. Besides, it's your child who will face the consequences, not you.

how to survive a meeting with the principal

HOW TO SURVIVE
THE PROM

IF A DATE CANCELS

If your teen's date cancels, put as many of the following plans into simultaneous action as possible to find a replacement date.

⭐ Cruise local hotels and event venues.
Phone to determine what other formal events are taking place that night, then visit the locales to find a suitable date. Weddings, bar and bat mitzvahs, and charity balls are good events to troll. Avoid 50th anniversary parties.

⭐ Start a phone chain with family and friends.
Cousins, family friends, and neighbors are the most likely candidates, as are foreign exchange students and visitors from out of town.

⭐ Check formalwear stores.
An employee in a formalwear store may already be dressed and ready to go.

⭐ Order pizzas from several different pizza establishments.
Select the most attractive delivery person. Tip well.

⭐ Hire an escort.
Find as reputable an entertainment service or modeling agency as possible. Do not tip well.

IF YOU HAVE TO DRIVE

1 Disguise yourself.
Wear a wig, chauffeur's cap, paste-on mustache, thick glasses, fake nose, or other identity-changing device. Protect your identity, not only for your teen's sake, but also for your own.

2 Alter the appearance of your car.
Make your car look more like a car service vehicle. Create a sign that reads "Professional Limo Service" and place it in the window. Place a small cooler with sodas and snacks in the back seat. Tape small signs on the back of the driver's and passenger's seats that say, "Do not talk to driver," and "Tipping permitted." If possible, borrow a friend's or family member's luxury sedan.

3 Speak in a cultivated, sophisticated accent.
Address your child and the date formally as "Sir" or "Miss."

4 Do not talk to your passengers.
Do not join the conversational flow. Even if there is awkward silence in the back seat, do not fill the gap with musings of your own prom and teenage exploits.

5 Resist the urge to act parentally.
Even if you see behavior you know to be inappropriate, restrain yourself from interjecting unless the law is being broken or lives are being threatened. You are the driver, not the parent. Discuss only pick-up times and wait times.

How to Avoid a Corsage Wound

Pin the corsage on your daughter's dress to save her date from embarrassment and her from injury. If it is your son going to the prom, instruct him on how to proceed.

1 Remove the corsage from its box.

2 Watch out for the long pin.
There will be at least one pin piercing the flower or stem.

3 Remove the pin(s) from the corsage.

4 Position the corsage so that the flowers point up.

5 Determine the best location for the corsage.
The ideal location for the corsage depends upon what the woman is wearing: Usually, it should be pinned on the dress near the collarbone, so that she can turn her head slightly to smell the flowers. Do not pin the corsage so high that her chin hits the flowers when she moves her head. If she is wearing a strapless dress, pin the corsage at her waist or on her evening bag.

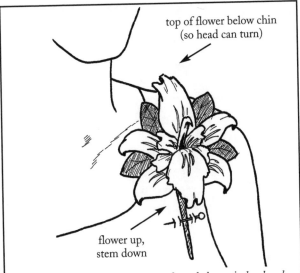

top of flower below chin
(so head can turn)

flower up,
stem down

Insert pin through dress, over stem, through dress; pin head and point finish outside dress.

6 Pin the corsage to the fabric.

Gently pull the fabric away from her body, or slide your fingers, palm out, between the dress and her skin. Insert the pin horizontally (toward her skin), then back through fabric (away from her skin) and over the corsage stem to hold it in place. Complete the pinning by running the pin once more through the fabric (toward her skin) and back out again (away from her skin). You will have made four holes in her dress.

Be Aware
Remember to move the tip of the pin to the outside of her dress for its final resting place.

HOW TO SURVIVE EMPTY-NEST SYNDROME

1 Allow yourself time to grieve.
Sadness is a natural reaction to your child's departure. Permit yourself to cry now and again without shame.

2 Find a temporary replacement for your affection.
To ease the transition, get a pet, or take your child's photo to a copy center and get a life-sized replica.

3 Wean yourself.
- Rearrange furniture in your entire house, not just in your child's room. A new look can make you feel like you have entered a new stage of life.
- Remove the most recent photos of your child. Recent photos can be a reminder that he was recently in the house—replace them with older images.
- Establish a "Reminder Jar." Similar to a "Swearing Jar" into which a parent places money for every swearing infraction, this jar reinforces behavior modification and punishes "remember when" infractions.

4 Convert your child's room into your own space.
Install a Murphy or sofa bed so that your child will have a place to stay when he comes home for visits, but alter the primary function of the room permanently. Set up a home theater, exercise room, or greenhouse.

Return to your pre-child life.

 Return to your pre-child life.
- Read a book.
- Invite your friends over for dinner.
- Fire the maid.
- Enjoy the quiet and calm.
- Watch the television shows you want to watch.
- Find things just where you left them.
- Take a trip.

Be Aware
Keep a list of the things your child did that annoyed, frustrated, and angered you. When you start to recall these things with fondness and a smile, you will have successfully entered the next phase of your life.

HOW TO SURVIVE
IF YOUR CHILD
MOVES BACK IN

⭐ Be sensitive to your child's needs—for a while.
Sometimes a child returns home because of a negative life change. Be understanding, and realize that a child moving back home is a difficult situation for all involved. Do not let yourself be exploited, however.

⭐ Charge rent.
Match market rates—deep discounting will only encourage your child to stay where it's cheap and easy.

⭐ Assign chores.
More people means more work, so delegate laundry folding, mowing the lawn, cleaning the porches, washing dishes, raking leaves, and other tasks. Do not offer to pay an allowance. If other family members have also moved in—your son- or daughter-in-law or grandchildren—give them chores as well.

⭐ Motivate change.
Place the classified advertisements section of the newspaper by your child's door. Do not change the message on your answering machine. Do not provide him with meals, change his bed linens, or allow him to watch television in the family room.

⭐ Do not alter your new lifestyle.
Continue to host your book group, bridge club, and cocktail parties. Continue to use his old room for its new purpose—sewing, exercising, big screen television watching.

How to Prevent Reentry

⭐ Change the locks.
Change the alarm code, too.

⭐ Paint the house.
He might not recognize an unfamiliar color.

⭐ Hide the car.
Park around the corner.

⭐ Put a different name on the door/mailbox.

⭐ Get a large, unfriendly pet.
Any size dog or cat can be effective if he is allergic.

⭐ Move to a smaller place.

⭐ Disappear.
Go on an extended vacation, rent an RV, or simply move out of town. Turn off your cell phone. Do not leave a forwarding address.

Put a different name on the mailbox.

Get a large unfriendly pet.

new lock

Change the locks.

Disappear.

Be Aware
Parenting is forever.

APPENDIX

ESSENTIAL PARENTAL CLICHÉS

When I was your age, we . . .
Because you're the child and I'm the parent.
Life isn't fair.
When you're the parent, you'll make the rules.
They call it bedtime for a reason.
Do I have to come up/in/over there?
You're bored? I'm Dad, nice to meet you.
Just a few more minutes/miles.
Don't make me tell you again.
That's twice. Three strikes and you're out.
You make a better door than a window.
Eat your vegetables.
So, I guess you don't like dessert anymore?
Because it's my house.
Because it's my car.
Because I'm the parent.
Just because.
There's no allowance without "allow."
I can't wait until you have kids.
Can you keep the noise down to a dull roar?
Are you trying to heat/cool the entire
    neighborhood?
Money doesn't grow on trees.
I'll give you something to cry about.
Maybe.
You'll spoil your dinner.
Find something to do.

Do you have something you want to tell me about?
You won't be happy until someone loses an eye.
If [*fill in blank*] jumped off a bridge, would you?
I hope your kids are just like you.
When I was your age, we didn't have . . .
This is why we can't have nice things.
You're not going out looking like that.
No son/daughter of mine is . . .
This is going to hurt me more than it hurts you.
Do you want to catch pneumonia?
I do and do and do for you kids and this is the
    thanks I get.
This is why I have gray hair.
You have nothing to do? I'll give you something
    to do.
There are children starving in . . .
Because it's good for you.
Don't make me ask you again.
The food left on your plate could feed a small
    village in . . .
Your face is going to stay like that.
Too bad, so sad.
Go to your room to cry.
Because I said so.
While you're under my roof, you follow my rules.
Children should be seen and not heard.
Don't make me pull this car over.
Go ask your mother/father.

"BIRDS-AND-BEES" SPEECH

Son/Daughter, I think you're old enough now to understand some things about Nature and how we all got here. It's best that you hear about these things from me and not from the kids at school who might not understand everything. I'll explain things to you, and you can talk to me without feeling embarrassed.

You've noticed that there are differences between boys and girls, between moms and dads, and soon you will notice that your body is changing. These changes are normal, and have to do with hormones that your body produces. These hormones and changes are the way your body gets ready to become an adult and to be able to make a baby.

It takes both a man and a woman to make a baby, just the way it takes a male dog and a female dog to make puppies. The female has a litter, which means she gives birth to several tiny puppies at the same time. Other animals have babies by laying eggs, but it still takes a male chicken, called a rooster, and a female chicken, called a hen, to produce eggs that have chicks inside. Hens can produce eggs without a rooster, like the eggs we have for breakfast, but those eggs aren't fertilized, which means that they don't have a chick inside and they won't hatch. All birds lay eggs. Female bees and fish also lay eggs, but the way the male fertilizes the eggs is different.

I think that's enough for one day.

Any questions?

INSTANT-MESSAGING DECODER

Text Messaging Abbreviation	Translation
ASL (alternatively A/S/L)	Age, sex, location (posed as a question)
BF (alternatively B/F)	Boyfriend
BYOB	Bring your own bottle/booze
CIBM	Could it be magic?
4YEO	For your eyes only
GF (alternatively G/F)	Girlfriend
H4U	Hot for you
H&K	Hug and kiss
ILU (alternatively ILY)	I love you
IWALY	I will always love you
KOTC	Kiss on the cheek
LTR	Long-term relationship
MOSS	Member of same sex
MOOS	Member of opposite sex
POS	Parent over shoulder
PRL	Parents are listening
PRW	People are watching
QT	Cutie
SPST	Same place, same time
STR8	Straight
W8FME	Wait for me
YIWGP	Yes I will go private

GLOSSARY OF TEENAGE SLANG

WORD	MEANING
All up in my grill	Get in someone's face
Ape	Crazy
Ass	Anything displeasing
Bling-bling	Similar to flossin'; glamorous, to shine like a diamond
Bounce	Leave
Butta/money	Good
Chickenhead	Promiscuous girl
Dawg	Friend
Def	Definitely
Flossin'	Show off wealth or belongings
Fo sheazy	For sure
Gank/jack	Steal
Get your swerve on	Get drunk
Ghetto	Cheap, shoddy
Heezy	House
Hit it	Have sex
Hit me up	Call or page me
Holla	Greet or call

the worst-case scenario survival handbook: parenting

Glossary of Teenage Slang

Word	Meaning
Jacked	Messed up, stolen
Lights are on	Can't talk, parents are in the room
The Man/popo/5-0 (five-oh)	Police officer
M.I.L.F.	Attractive mom
Mos	Most
Off the hook	Fun, wild
Peeps	Friends
Pigeon	Ugly girl
Playa	Someone who is romantically involved with many people at the same time
Rents	Parents
Rocks	Big diamonds
Shot to the curb	Hung over/down and out
Skrilla/cheddar/cabbage/ dead presidents	Money
Spent	Tired
Spit game	Make a pass at someone
Stay up	See you later

THE EXPERTS

Colin C. Adams, Ph.D., is the Francis C. Oakley Third Century Professor of Mathematics at Williams College. He is the author of *The Knot Book: An Elementary Introduction to the Mathematical Theory of Knots,* used as the text in many knot theory courses, and the co-author of *How to Ace Calculus: The Streetwise Guide.*

American Academy of Pediatrics (www.aap.org).

Stevanne "Dr. Toy" Auerbach, Ph.D., is a child development specialist and the author of 15 books, including *FAO Schwarz Toys for a Lifetime: Enhancing Childhood Through Play* and *Dr. Toy's Smart Play: How to Raise a Child with a High PQ.* Her website, www.drtoy.com, provides year-round guidance on toys and play.

David G. Berkebile, D.C. (www.dcberk.com), treats posture-related problems in Johnstown, Pennsylvania, and works closely with Backpack Safety for Kids, an international organization. He is a frequent lecturer on posture, backpack safety, nutrition, and healthy lifestyles.

Amy L. Best is assistant professor of Sociology at San Jose State University. She is the author of *Prom Night: Youth, Schools, and Popular Culture.*

Marybeth Bond (www.womentraveltips.com) is a travel expert/spokesperson, motivational speaker, commentator, mother of two, and the author of five books, including *A Woman's World, Gutsy Women,* and *Gutsy Mamas.*

Chad Boonswang is a Philadelphia attorney who has deposed and cross-examined hundreds of witnesses in civil and criminal cases.

Brent W. Bost, M.D., a fellow of the American College of Obstetricians and Gynecologists, has a private medical practice in Beaumont, Texas, and has delivered more than 7,000 babies. He is the author of *The Hurried Woman* (www.hurriedwoman.com).

Eileen Buckholtz and her son, Ryan, are the creators of www.TeenDriving.com, an award-winning website and community service project dedicated to promoting safe teen driving and saving lives.

Kathleen Burklow is a psychologist at the Cincinnati Children's Hospital Medical Center. She is an assistant professor at Children's Hospital Medical Center, Division of Psychology, University of Cincinnati.

Dominic Cappello designs safety, health, and communications programs for parents and educators, and is the author of *Ten Talks About Violence* and the co-author of *Ten Talks About Sex and Character* and *Ten Talks About Drugs and Choices* (www.tentalks.com). He is currently developing an animated television series.

Amy Chezem is the director of public relations for the National Association of Chewing Gum Manufacturers (www.nacgm.org).

Edward R. Christophersen, Ph.D., is a staff psychologist at Children's Mercy Hospital in Kansas City, Missouri, and a professor of pediatrics at the University of Missouri at Kansas City School of Medicine. He is the author of *Parenting That Works*.

Karen S. Deerwester, Ed.S., is the founder and CEO of Family Time Inc. (www.familytimeinc.com), a parent-child coaching and consulting firm. Since 1984, she has trained early childhood teachers, developed and operated parent/child centers, and supported thousands of parents and teachers through parent/child classes, professional seminars, and one-to-one coaching.

Anita Dunham-Potter is a travel writer, former flight attendant, and mother of two. She writes magazine articles and publishes a newsletter on traveling with (and occasionally without) kids, available from her website, www.AnitaVacation.com.

Warren Eckstein (www.warreneckstein.com) has worked with animals for 30 years and is the author of 11 books, including *Memoirs of a Pet Therapist* and *How to Get Your Dog to Do What You Want*. His radio program, *The Pet Show with Warren Eckstein*, is syndicated in 90 markets, and he is the contributing pet editor on the *Today* show.

Kandy Ferriby owns The Doll Company (www.4theloveofdolls.com), a shop that specializes in the professional repair and restoration of antique and modern dolls. She lives in Texas.

Alan Fierstein, president of Acoustilog, Inc. (www.acoustilog.com), provides professional acoustic measurement, acoustic and noise consultation, and soundproofing design and troubleshooting services in New York City.

Chuck Fresh (www.chuckfresh.com) is a DJ and the author of *How to Be a DJ: Your Guide to Becoming a Radio, Nightclub or Private Party DJ*. He produces radio commercials and provides marketing consulting services for clubs and bars from his Florida home.

Mark Frey teaches computer science at Skyline High School in Oakland, California. He began keeping a record of teen slang in 1995 and maintains an online dictionary of Oakland teen slang at www.voxcommunications.com.

Jacqueline Haines is the director of the Gesell Institute of Human Development and co-author of *School Readiness* and *The Gesell Institute's Child from One to Six*.

Charles Henderson, Ph.D., is an Assistant Professor of Physics at Western Michigan University.

Joan Holub (www.joanholub.com) is the author/illustrator of more than 50 children's books, including *Eek-A-Boo! A Spooky Lift-the-Flap Book*, *Tatiana Comes to America*, and *The Garden That We Grew*.

Alice Sterling Honig, Ph.D., is professor emerita, Child Development Studies, Syracuse University. She is the author of numerous books on raising children, including *Behavior Guidance for Infants and Toddlers* and *Secure Relationships: Nurturing Infant-Toddler Attachment in Early Care Settings*.

Ron Huxley (www.parentingtoolbox.com), a licensed child and family therapist, anger management expert, and father of four, is the author of *Love & Limits: Achieving a Balance in Parenting*.

Harriet Joseph, Ed.D., is associate director of the University Scholars Program in the Center for Undergraduate Research and Fellowships at the University of Pennsylvania. She is a mother of two, and the former host of an exchange student.

Ken Kaiser, who has worked in the toy industry for 30 years, is president of KidCo, a Mundelein, Illinois–based company that specializes in the marketing, distribution, and manufacturing of upscale children's products.

Janis Keyser is a teacher, parent educator, program director, and speaker who specializes in early childhood and family development. She is the co-author of *Becoming the Parent You Want to Be: A Sourcebook of Strategies for the First Five Years* (www.becomgingtheparent.com). She teaches at Cabrillo College in Aptos, California, and has been conducting workshops for parents and teachers for more than 30 years.

Melisa W. Lai, M.D., is a clinical chief resident in Emergency Medicine at the Harvard Affiliated Emergency Medicine Residency Program at Massachusetts General Hospital-Brigham & Women's Hospital-Mt.Auburn.

James Li, M.D., practices and teaches in the Division of Emergency Medicine at Harvard Medical School in Cambridge, Massachusetts. He is an instructor for the American College of Surgeons' course for physicians, Advanced Trauma Life Support.

Eric Lombardini, V.M.D., is a captain in the U.S. Army Veterinary Corps. He commands a veterinary medical detachment responsible for the care of military working dogs and other government-owned animals.

Jim Maas, Ph.D., a professor of psychology and sleep educator at Cornell University, coaches professional and Olympic athletes on effective sleep techniques. He is the author of the best-selling *Power Sleep*, as well as the children's book *Remmy and the Brain Train*. He maintains a website on sleep for children at www.remmyweb.com.

Richard Meischeid is a Philadelphia consultant, volunteer soccer coach, and father of two athletic children involved in many sports leagues.

Steven Miller, M.D., is the director of Pediatric Emergency Medicine at New York Presbyterian Hospital.

Vinny Minchillo, a demolition derby driver for 20 years, has written for *AutoWeek*, *Sports Car*, and *Turbo* magazines. When not crashing cars, he is an advertising executive in Texas.

Dr. Jodi Mindell, Ph.D., is the associate director of the Center for Sleep Disorders at Children's Hospital of Philadelphia. She served as chair of the National Sleep Foundation's committee on newborn sleep (www.sleepfoundation.org) and is the author of *Sleeping Through the Night: How Infants, Toddlers, and Their Parents Can Get a Good Night's Sleep* and *Sleep, Your Baby, and You: Best Sleep Practices*.

Janet Mullington, Ph.D., an assistant professor of Neurology at Harvard Medical School, is director of the Human Sleep and Chronobiology Research Unit at the Beth Israel Deaconess Medical Center and the mother of twins.

Susan Newman, Ph.D. (www.susannewmanphd.com), is a social psychologist, parenting expert, and the author of numerous books, including *Nobody's Baby Now: Reinventing Your Adult Relationship with Your Mother and Father* and *Parenting an Only Child: The Joys and Challenges of Raising Your One and Only*.

Monica Pacheco-Zech (www.monicazech.com), public information officer and safety educator for the El Cajon Fire Department in El Cajon, California, spent 18 years as a television and radio traffic reporter. She lectures on driving, traffic safety, and injury prevention.

Don Rabon (www.donrabon.net), manager of the Investigations Center for the North Carolina Justice Academy, has trained investigators in interviewing and interrogation techniques in 47 states. He has also trained members of the U.S. military and Secret Service, the CIA, and NATO forces.

Bill Ranger is the fourth-generation owner of Macklem's Baby Carriages & Toys in Toronto (www.macklems.com), which specializes in the repair and restoration of strollers, baby carriages, and antique prams. He has been repairing carriages for 40 years.

Jeff Raz (www.jeffraz.com) has worked in circuses as a clown, acrobat, and juggler and in theater as an actor, director, and playwright. He is currently the director of the Clown Conservatory at the Circus Center, San Francisco (www.circuscenter.org).

Adelaide Robb, M.D., is a pediatrician in the psychiatry department at Children's National Medical Center in the District of Columbia.

Gail M. Saltz, M.D., is chairman of Public Information for the New York Psychoanalytic Institute and an assistant professor of psychiatry at New York Presbyterian Hospital, Weill-Cornell Medical Center. She has a private practice in New York City and is the mental health contributor for the *Today* show.

Ellyn Satter (www.ellynsatter.com) is a family therapist, dietitian, and author based in Madison, Wisconsin. She is the author of *Child of Mine: Feeding with Love and Good Sense; Secrets of Feeding a Healthy Family;* and *How to Get Your Kid to Eat . . . But Not Too Much.*

Lawrence B. Schiamberg is an associate dean and professor of Family and Child Ecology at Michigan State University in East Lansing. He is co-author of *The Encyclopedia of Human Ecology* and the author of numerous books and scholarly articles on human development, child and adolescent development, aging, and retirement.

Lisa Schulman (www.LisaShulman.com) is a parenting journalist who has contributed to iVillage, momsonline.com, *Parents* magazine, and kidshealth.org.

Hugh Shelton owns First Shot Photo and Carriage (www.firstshotphoto.com), a shop that specializes in the restoration and repair of antique wagons and wagon wheels. He lives in Gonzales, Texas.

Joan Elizabeth Shook, M.D., is chief of Emergency Medicine Service at Texas Children's Hospital in Houston, and serves as an associate professor of Pediatrics and chief of Pediatric Emergency Medicine at Baylor College of Medicine.

Myrna B. Shure, Ph.D., a developmental psychologist and Professor of Developmental Psychology at Drexel University, is the author of *Raising a Thinking Child* and *Raising a Thinking Preteen.* She creates curricula for schools and trains educators and parents in effective child development strategies.

John Simonetti is an astronomer and associate professor of physics at Virginia Tech in Blacksburg, Virginia.

Lorena Siqueiro, M.D., is a pediatrician at Miami Children's Hospital specializing in adolescent medicine.

Laurel Smith, a former teacher, runs www.Momsminivan.com, a resource for parents on travel games and road trip ideas. She has logged thousands of driving miles with her three children. She lives in Louisiana.

Paul Soven is a professor at the University of Pennsylvania who studies theoretical condensed-matter physics. He has served as associate chair of both undergraduate and graduate affairs in the physics department and has published numerous articles on the electronic structure of materials.

Gary Sowatzka, a doll doctor with 20 years of experience, has repaired thousands of dolls with restoration techniques that include bisque, papier-mâché, composition, felt, cloth, and hard plastics. He answers questions on dolls and doll repair from his website, www.sowatzka.com.

Maxine Sprague, B.Ed., is a parent, educator, and author of three books, including *Super Easy Bag Lunches*. She lives in Alberta, Canada, with her family.

Dr. Robert W. Steele is a noted author and practicing pediatrician at St. John's Children's Hospital in Springfield, Missouri. He has contributed to Parentsplace.com and *On the Safe Side: Your Complete Reference to Childproofing for Infants and Toddlers*, among other publications.

Bridget Swinney, M.S., R.D., is the author of *Eating Expectantly* and *Healthy Food for Healthy Kids* (www.healthyfoodzone.com). She is a nutrition expert in the field of prenatal and child nutrition and family eating issues.

Robin Thompson founded the Etiquette-Network (www.etiquette-network.com) in 1983 and lectures on etiquette and image for all ages at schools, universities, and businesses. She is the author of *Be the Best You Can Be: A Guide to Etiquette and Self-Improvement for Children and Teens*.

Judith Turow, M.D., is an assistant professor of Pediatrics at Thomas Jefferson University in Philadelphia and was named a "Top Doc" by *Philadelphia Magazine*.

David Ufberg, M.D., is an obstetrician and gynecologist at Pennsylvania Hospital, an assistant professor in the University of Pennsylvania Health System, and a father. He has delivered thousands of babies.

Penny Warner (www.pennywarner.com) is the author of *Slumber Parties* and numerous other party books for children.

James M. Watt, C.M.L., C.P.S., has been a locksmith since 1975. He co-founded the Montana Locksmiths Association and has served on the Associated Locksmiths of America (ALOA) Board of Directors and as Northwest Vice President.

Lennard Zinn (www.zinncycles.com), a bike racer, framebuilder, and technical writer, was a member of the U.S. Olympic Development (road) Cycling Team and is the author of *Zinn and the Art of Road Bike Maintenance, Zinn and the Art of Mountain Bike Maintenance, Mountain Bike Performance Handbook,* and *Mountain Bike Owner's Manual.*

ABOUT THE AUTHORS

JOSHUA PIVEN stayed out past curfew, occasionally skipped class, and was once stuffed into a locker. He still has temper tantrums and avoids brussels sprouts, but is rarely robbed of his lunch money. He is the co-author, with David Borgenicht, of the *Worst-Case Scenario Survival Handbook* series.

DAVID BORGENICHT is the co-author of all the books in the *Worst-Case Scenario Survival Handbook* series, and the co-parent of a beautiful daughter, Sophie. He has survived sleep deprivation, diaper disasters, and airplane mishaps galore. He lives in Philadelphia.

SARAH JORDAN is a National Magazine Award nominee and writer living in Philadelphia with her husband, Jon, and son, Charles. She is a survivor of induced labor, mommy groups, nanny searches, and debates on issues such as tummy time and binky addiction.

BRENDA BROWN is a freelance illustrator and cartoonist whose work has been published in many books and major publications, including *The Worst-Case Scenario Survival Handbook* series, *Esquire*, *Reader's Digest*, *USA Weekend*, *21st Century Science & Technology*, *The Saturday Evening Post*, *The National Enquirer*, and many other magazines. Her work has also appeared in specialized education series, websites, and promotional ad campaigns. Brenda's website: http://webtoon.com.

Check out www.worstcasescenarios.com for updates, new scenarios, and more! Because you just never know . . .

Acknowledgments

Josh Piven thanks the experts for their sage advice and great humor during the writing of the book. May their kids appreciate their wisdom as much!

David Borgenicht would like to thank his editors, Jay Schaefer, Melissa Wagner, and Steve Mockus, for their creative minds and critical eyes; Frances J. Soo Ping Chow for her graphic expertise and hair; and the entire staff at Quirk Books and Chronicle Books for just being there. Above all, he'd like to acknowledge the experts who contributed their knowledge to this work (your efforts will no doubt save the lives of beleagured parents everywhere), his wife, Suzanne (he really couldn't have done this without HER), and his daughter, Sophie (who taught him everything he knows about parenting—the old-fashioned way).

Sarah Jordan thanks all the pediatricians and parenting experts; she also thanks her family and the team of babysitters—Barbara "Grandma" Jordan, Andrea Torzone, Jessica Capizzi, and Rebecca Kenton— who gave this mom the time to work. Finally, unending gratitude and love go to super-dad and husband, Jon, and adorable research assistant, son Charles.

MORE WORST-CASE SCENARIOS